MIRROR OF OBEDIENCE

ALSO AVAILABLE FROM BLOOMSBURY

Venice Saved, edited and translated by Silvia Caprioglio Panizza
and Philip Wilson
The Religious Philosophy of Simone Weil, by Lissa McCullough
Simone Weil, by Mario von der Ruhr

MIRROR OF OBEDIENCE

The Poems and Selected Prose of Simone Weil

Edited and translated by

SILVIA CAPRIOGLIO PANIZZA
AND PHILIP WILSON

BLOOMSBURY ACADEMIC
LONDON • NEW YORK • OXFORD • NEW DELHI • SYDNEY

BLOOMSBURY ACADEMIC
Bloomsbury Publishing Plc
50 Bedford Square, London, WC1B 3DP, UK
1385 Broadway, New York, NY 10018, USA
29 Earlsfort Terrace, Dublin 2, Ireland

BLOOMSBURY, BLOOMSBURY ACADEMIC and the Diana logo are trademarks
of Bloomsbury Publishing Plc

First published in Great Britain 2023

Cover design by Maria Rajka
Cover image: Painting titled 'Fog on the Sea'. Oil on canvas.
(© World History Archive / Alamy Stock Photo)

A catalogue record for this book is available from the British Library.

A catalog record for this book is available from the Library of Congress.

ISBN: HB: 978-1-3502-5067-3
PB: 978-1-3502-5068-0
ePDF: 978-1-3502-5069-7
eBook: 978-1-3502-5070-3

Typeset by Deanta Global Publishing Services, Chennai, India
Printed and bound in Great Britain

To find out more about our authors and books visit www.bloomsbury.com and
sign up for our newsletters.

Sea, docile at ebb. Sea, slave to the silence.
Sparse sea, chained for eternity to the flows.
Mass open to sky, mirror of obedience.
The distant stars, effortlessly, have the power
to weave into you every night these new folds.
Simone Weil, 'The Sea'

CONTENTS

Biographies	ix
Preface	xi
On the translation	xiv
Acknowledgements	xvii
List of abbreviations	xix

1 Simone Weil as poet   1

2 Simone Weil and literature   45

Poems   83

    À une jeune fille riche/To a Rich Girl   84

    Vers lus au Goûter de la Saint Charlemagne/

       Verses Read at the Feast of Saint Charlemagne   90

    Éclair/Lightning   100

    Prométhée/Prometheus   102

    À un jour/To a Day   108

    La mer/The Sea   122

    Nécessité/Necessity   124

    Les astres/The Stars   126

    La porte/The Gate   128

Four excerpts from *Venice Saved*   131

    Jaffier 1–3   132

    Violetta   138

Selected prose   141
      Conte: Les Lutins du feu/Tale: The Fairies of the Fire   142
      Le conte des six cygnes dans Grimm/The Tale of the
        Six Swans in Grimm   148

Notes   157
Further reading   167
Bibliography   168
Index   175

BIOGRAPHIES

Silvia Caprioglio Panizza and Philip Wilson have translated and edited Simone Weil's verse tragedy *Venice Saved* (Bloomsbury 2019).

Silvia Caprioglio Panizza is Marie Skłodowska-Curie Fellow at the Centre for Ethics, University of Pardubice, working on a project on moral impossibility (MIGHT), and a member of PEriTiA, Centre for Ethics in Public Life, University College Dublin, Dublin, Ireland. She is the author of *The Ethics of Attention: Engaging the Real with Iris Murdoch and Simone Weil* (Routledge 2022) and co-editor of *The Murdochian Mind* (with Mark Hopwood, Routledge 2022). Her research focuses on meta-ethics, moral psychology, environmental ethics and animal ethics. She is the leader of the Vegan Studies Network (VSN).

Philip Wilson is Associate Professor of Philosophy and Translation at the University of East Anglia, Norwich, UK. Academic publications include *Literary Translation: Redrawing the Boundaries* (edited with Jean Boase-Beier and Antoinette Fawcett, Palgrave Macmillan 2014), *Translation after Wittgenstein* (Routledge 2016) and *The Routledge Handbook* *of Translation and Philosophy* (edited with Piers Rawling, Routledge 2018). Translations include *The Luther Breviary* (with John Gledhill, Wartburg 2007), *The Bright Rose: German Verse 800–1280* (Arc Publications 2015), *Alexander Neville's Norwich Histories* (with Ingrid Walton and Clive Wilkins-Jones, Boydell 2019) and *Karl Marx: Evening Hour* (Arc Publications 2022). He is currently working on a monograph on translation and mysticism (Routledge).

PREFACE

Simone Weil (1909–43) is recalled and read as a philosopher and mystic who addresses political, ethical and metaphysical questions. Jewish by birth, she was passionately drawn to Catholicism but was unable to take the step of becoming a member of the Church by baptism, in the conviction that too much truth lay outside Christianity for her to commit to it, and because, out of love, she preferred to remain among the outsiders of the world. She also viewed the Church as totalitarian and 'sullied by a host of crimes' (LP 23). Among her major writings (in English translation from French) are *Letter to a Priest*, *Oppression and Liberty*, *The Need for Roots* and *Waiting for God*. Interest in her thought continues to grow.

Weil was passionate about literature. She read widely and worked on poems and a verse tragedy, though her output has received little attention. Her play remained unpublished in English until it appeared as *Venice Saved* in our translation from Bloomsbury in 2019. The current volume is a companion to that edition and offers both the poems and verse extracts from the play, a story written when Weil was eleven years old and an essay about a Grimm tale composed while preparing for university entrance. The corpus of poetry is small, only nine poems, but nobody is deterred from reading (say) Sappho just because we do not have many of her lyrics. If Weil had lived longer, she would in all likelihood have finished her play and written more verse. As it was, she died aged thirty-four. Weil's life story has influenced a number of poets, including Anne Carson, Jorie Graham, Seamus Heaney, Geoffrey Hill, Czesław Miłosz and Rebecca Tamás, so it is not surprising that she should have felt inspired to write verse about what she went through.

Weil's own literary work was important to her. She was writing and re-working her poems and her play until the end; in a letter to her parents from London of 22 January 1943, she indicated changes to be made to various texts and expressed the hope that her verses would appear in print together in chronological order (SL 168), a wish fulfilled by Gallimard's 1955 edition of *Poèmes suivis de Venise sauvée* [Poems followed by Venice Saved], which was reissued in 1968 but is now generally unavailable. The poetry and the play will be republished as part of Gallimard's ongoing project of issuing the complete works.

To read Weil's poems in order is to progress through her life and thought, as we show in the introductory Chapter 1 on Weil as poet, which is followed by Chapter 2 on Weil as reader. Our English translations then appear opposite the French source texts. We see bilingual presentation as a major strength of this book. Readers with French can refer to Weil's originals, while all readers can make comparisons between the French and the

English, even if only at the level of comparing the shapes of poems or tracking key vocabulary. The translations are written to stand on their own as verse or prose while representing what Weil wrote. We have commented on our translation strategy and have provided notes for each text. It is our hope that this edition will shed light on the life and the thought of one of the twentieth century's great prophets, as well as offering literature worth reading in its own right. Weil's work has been to a large extent a project of scholarly reconstruction because most of what she wrote was unpublished in her lifetime. The appearance of her poetry in English will contribute to the building of the mosaic.

The translation has been completed as humanity reels from global epidemic, climate change and war. Weil, whose last years were spent as a fugitive from Nazism, can through her literary output offer solace and consolation to an afflicted world and also issue a challenge to start again and to do better. As Megan Nolan wrote at the beginning of the pandemic:

The philosopher Simone Weil believed that paying attention was the most fundamental of our obligations, the least of what we owe to each other. In paying attention we honour the suffering that binds us all. (2021)

ON THE TRANSLATION

Literature – whether verse, prose or drama – heightens language by employing it in new ways. Authors draw attention to the mode of telling and impose stylistic patterns on their material, such as rhyme, alliteration, repetition, imagery or personification. Derek Attridge argues that literary works are therefore translatable because their singularity can be imitated in the target text (2004: 76). In our translation, we imitate the singularity of Simone Weil.

A plain prose translation of the poems could have been given, which would have allowed the reader to access Weil's ideas, but we decided to write versions that would work as poems in English. Form and content are indivisible in verse and these texts mattered to Simone Weil *as poetry*. The work that we have imitated is highly traditional and uses full rhyme, strict rhyme schemes and set numbers of syllables per line, including the twelve-syllable Alexandrine, which is used by Weil in 'To a Rich Girl', for example.[1] Weil writes that poetic constraints such as rhyme 'impose upon the poet a direction in his choice of words which is absolutely unrelated to the sequence of ideas', so that the function of rhyme in poetry is 'perhaps analogous

---

[1]French formal verse is based on numbers of syllables rather than on stresses: for an overview, see Rees (1980: xxix–xxxv).

to that of affliction in our lives' (WG 113).[2] The form mirrors the content. Thus Joan Dargan remarks that Weil calls attention in 'Necessity' to the poem's 'imperfection' by writing in lines of eleven syllables, an 'odd, disjointed meter' that falls one syllable short of the classical Alexandrine (1999: 91); what is disjointed in French remains disjointed in our translation.

We have also maintained Weil's formalism by, for example, using rhyme and writing lines with the same numbers of syllables as the source text in order to signal, as we did in our translation of *Venice Saved*, that 'we are offering a representation of a very different way of writing poetry' (VS 44). We have used a variety of rhyming techniques – assonance and consonance as well as full rhyme – because English is less rhyme-rich than French. Weil's poems are appearing together for the first time in English translation; therefore, it would be premature to write very free or experimental renderings, by, say, translating Weil in the manner of George Herbert (which remains an interesting future possibility). We have followed practice in contemporary English poetry by not automatically capitalizing at the start of lines (as Weil does), as an aid to flow, but we have used capital letters in titles (such as 'The Stars' for 'Les astres'), again in line with (most) contemporary English practice. Even such small

---

[2]For the case that constraint can be a cause of literary creativity in both source and target text, see Boase-Beier and Holman (1999).

matters of presentation indicate how translation is never a matter of quasi-mathematical transference but involves choice and can always be done in other ways, because every translation is an interpretation.

The two prose pieces are very different in tone from the poems and from each other: a fairy story and an academic essay about a folktale. We have written English target texts that respond to the voice of the source in each case but that again can be read independently of Weil. 'The Fairies of the Fire' is composed with a sense of wonder, in a revelatory voice, while 'The Tale of the Six Swans in Grimm' sums up a canonical fairy tale, comments on it and moves to a radical Platonic conclusion, thus using three distinct voices. As Simon Armitage argues, 'the job of the translator is to create a plausible universe' (2021: 223). Thus, for example, the names of the characters in the story of the Fairies have been retained in Greek form but have lost the accents used by Weil.

The first poem in *Mirror of Obedience*, 'To a Rich Girl', is appearing in English one hundred years after it was written in French. We hope that our work obediently mirrors the universe created by Weil and that she continues to find new readers who will take her vision further.

ACKNOWLEDGEMENTS

Many thanks to Davide Rizza for first suggesting that we look at the literary Weil and for his constant encouragement in our two translation projects, and to the following for their generous support: Gareth Jones, Kate Lawton and Stephen Spencer. Jean Boase-Beier has given us invaluable advice on the nature of poetry and its translation, which has influenced our discussion about the quality of Weil's verse in Chapter 1. We are very grateful to Liza Thompson and Lucy Russell, our wonderful editors at Bloomsbury, who have been with us every step of the way, and we also thank Bloomsbury's five anonymous reviewers for their very insightful comments on the first and the final draft of the manuscript. Any errors are, of course, our own.

The source texts, with one exception, are taken from the 1968 Gallimard edition *Poèmes suivis de Venise sauvée, Lettre de Paul Valéry*, which includes a valuable (anonymous) editor's note and Paul Valéry's letter to Weil of 20 September 1937. The essay 'Le conte des six cygnes dans Grimm' can be found in Florence de Lussy's edition of Weil's *Œuvres* (O 803–4).

De Lussy offers a useful chronology and a selection of Weil's autobiographical writings and letters (1999), on which we have drawn for our discussion of Weil's life in Chapter 1, along with

Richard Rees's *Seventy Letters* (1965) and biographical work by Gabriella Fiori (1989), Simone Pétrement (1976), Stephen Plant (2007) and Palle Yourgrau (2011). We found Thomas R. Nevin's discussion of the poetry very helpful (1991: 157–67) as well as Marie Cabaud Meaney (2007) on the classics and J. P. Little (1996) on language.

'The Gate', our translation of Weil's 'La porte', first appeared in a slightly different version in *Modern Poetry in Translation* (No. 1 2021). We have also used the commentary that we wrote to accompany it. Many thanks to that important journal and its editor Clare Pollard.

 Funded by the European Union

This project has received funding from the European Union's Horizon 2020 research and innovation programme under the Marie Skłodowska-Curie grant agreement No 101026701

ABBREVIATIONS

We reference Simone Weil's work in our editorial material by abbreviated title and page; thus (GG 50) is a reference to *Gravity and Grace* page 50. The Bibliography offers full details of the editions used. Weil's works are abbreviated as follows:

APP   *On the Abolition of All Political Parties* (2014)

FLN   *First and Last Notebooks* (1970)

GG   *Gravity and Grace* (2003)

GTG   *Gateway to God* (1982)

IC   *Intimations of Christianity among the Ancient Greeks* (1957)

IP   'The Iliad, or The Poem of Force' (2005)

LOP   *Lectures on Philosophy* (1978)

LP   *Letter to a Priest* (2002a)

LPW   *Late Philosophical Writings* (2015)

NB   *The Notebooks of Simone Weil* (1951)

NR   *The Need for Roots* (2002)

O   *Œuvres* (1999)

OL   *Oppression and Liberty* (2001)

PVS   *Poèmes suivis de Venise sauvée, Lettre de Paul Valéry* (1968)

PW   'The Power of Words' (2020)

RCV   'Some Reflections around the Concept of Value' (2014)

SL   *Seventy Letters* (1965)

SWA   *Simone Weil: An Anthology* (2005)

SWR   *Simone Weil Reader* (1977)

VS   *Venice Saved* (2019)

WG   *Waiting for God* (1973)

1

Simone Weil as poet

A life in poetry

To read Simone Weil is to have a personal encounter and to be forced to ask questions about this thinker, just as James Klagge notes that readers of Ludwig Wittgenstein's *Tractatus Logico-Philosophicus* cannot help wondering 'what kind of person its author was' because Wittgenstein's work exudes a feeling that it must be connected with the writer's life in some way (2001: ix). Chris Kraus calls Weil a 'performative philosopher' (2000: 26) and for Sarah Bakewell, she instantiates Iris Murdoch's claim that philosophy can be 'inhabited' (2016: 199). We argue in this chapter that Weil's poetry allows both her life and thought to be seen in a new refraction. Weil was always adamant that what mattered was the truth of what she wrote rather than what she did. As Lissa McCullough comments, there is reason to believe that she would have been 'intensely displeased' with a biographical approach to her philosophy (2014: 1), but we hold that literature must always be read in history, and therefore in this chapter we shall narrate Weil's life story *through* the poetry, so that life and work become mutually enlightening. We follow Ray Monk's view of the biographer's task:

> to enrich understanding in these two ways: by attending, so to speak, to the tone of voice in which a writer expresses himself or herself, and by accumulating personal facts that will allow us to see what is said in a different light. (2001: 4)

Monk's strategy is based on attention, which is a central theme in Weil's thinking, which she defines as follows:

> Attention consists of suspending our thought, leaving it detached, empty, and ready to be penetrated by the object. (WG 111)

Read in the context of her life, the poems can be seen as exercises in attention on Weil's part and can in turn become exercises in attention for the reader. Poetry is how Weil tells the truth obliquely, in line with Emily Dickinson's poetic injunction to tell 'all the truth but tell it slant' (1999: 494). Verse, after all, is not a left-aligned version of prose. As Wittgenstein remarks, a poem is not about giving information, even though it appears to be written in the language of giving information (*Zettel* 160). Weil wrote poetry to say what she could *not* say otherwise, in line with Stanley Cavell's assertion that for the philosopher to turn to literature is not to seek 'illustrations for truths philosophy already knows, but illumination of philosophical pertinence that philosophy alone has not surely grasped – as though an essential part of its task must work behind its back' (2002b: xxiv–xxv).

The question must be asked if Weil's poetry has any merit. Her philosophy teacher Alain dismissed her 1926 poem 'Charlemagne' as 'bad' (see later) and her work is not included in anthologies of French verse.[1] We make no claim that Weil is a great poet. However, the very concept of 'great poetry' is problematic, because it assumes that poetry is only one sort of thing, whereas it is many things, as poet Simon Armitage argues, even while he maintains that there is a 'golden standard' (2021: 273). Weil's lyrics are interesting in themselves, while not of the golden standard. And interesting poetry is important, as becomes apparent when editors set out to collect work around a theme, such as the Holocaust. Should only canonical Holocaust poets such as Paul Celan be included? In their recent anthology of Holocaust poetry, Jean Boase-Beier and Marian de Vooght aim 'to include poems by poets less well-known in the English-speaking world

---

[1] There are three texts by Weil in English translation in Roger Housden's anthology of mystical poetry (Housden 2009), but they are adaptations from her prose.

and to introduce some less familiar poems by poets who do not have an established name' (2019: 22). If the point is to show how different people reacted in verse to the Holocaust, then reputation cannot be the only criterion of admission, which implies that the canon can be extended. In the case of Weil, the issue is about the publication and translation of a figure who was not known for poetry because her career lay elsewhere. There are other figures in a similar position. The young Karl Marx, for example, dreamed of being a man of letters and penned more than one hundred poems before deciding to follow a political and philosophical vocation (see Marx 2022). He left interesting poetry that is worth reading both because of what it tells us about Marx and his world and also because at times it does show genuine poetic fire. Critics need to remain cautious about attributing greatness to any author on the basis of who they were but should not dismiss poets because they do not match the standards set by figures like Celan or because they did not make their name out of literature.

Again and again in Weil's poems is to be found the literary genius that characterizes her philosophical writing and that helps to make her a popular writer outside the academy. Deborah Nelson notes how reviewers have commented on the 'mathematical beauty of her prose; its clarity, balance, simplicity, transparency, and purity' (2017: 21). Weil herself had this to say about her poetry, in a note on her verse play *Venice Saved*:

The verses. They won't 'sound right' unless they create a new time for the reader. And as with music (Valéry) a poem emerges from silence, returns to silence.

Elements of the poem. A time that has a beginning and an end. To what does this correspond? Then the *flavour* of words: each word should have a maximal flavour between the sense ascribed to it and all its other senses; an agreement or an opposition with the sound of its syllables; agreements and oppositions with words before and after. (VS 57)

By paying attention to the formal quality of poetry, to the right choice of words, Weil aims to write verse that will capture the reader's attention.

For Weil scholars, the poems' main interest may lie in how they illustrate central themes in her philosophy: affliction, attention, beauty, grace, gravity, justice, necessity and obedience. These concepts emerge variously in different poems as traces of the development of a thinker, but there is one idea that runs through all the poems and indeed Weil's whole output: the existence of an objective order. The meaning and role of the themes mentioned depend on Weil's certainty that there is a reality, of which human beings are part, that is grounded in a realm at once material and metaphysical, which includes meaning, beauty and a moral structure. This certainty of an objective order is Platonic – for Weil there is 'nothing above

Plato' (SL 131) – and is given a Christian perspective in the later work.[2] Platonic elements emerge clearly and repeatedly in the poems, which assume the existence of a supernatural reality towards which humans strive. Full knowledge of it is unattainable, and the individual's aspiration towards the good is often misguided, but that is only due to the human condition. Our constant and primary duty – as Weil saw her own duty – is to tend towards that knowledge and to approximate our lives to the good. Roberto Carifi, philosopher, poet and translator of Weil, comments that her work has the rare ability to counter the nihilism of our times (1998: 7). Her vision is also at odds with the loss of metaphysics in the modern period through which she lived, as well as with the further fragmentation and erosion of the ideas of truth and meaning in the postmodern period, and with the current popularity of moral relativism and anti-realism in Western secular culture. For Weil, denying the existence of truth and forsaking the aspiration to something higher means not only to undermine all morality but also to turn away from the foundations of existence.

Weil wrote at a time of experimentation in French Literature, with poets pushing the boundaries of free verse, the prose poem, concrete poetry and surrealism. None of this is evident in her work, which, from her first attempt while

---

[2]See McCullough (2014: 214 ff.) for an account of theological influences on Weil.

still at school to the poems written shortly before her death and the verse of her play, is composed with mathematical precision to emulate traditional models. Her letters show how seriously she took her work. She revised constantly (cf. SL 167–8), shared poems with friends and sought a mentor in poet and intellectual Paul Valéry, who is mentioned by her in the foregoing quotation (see also WG 168) and whose symbolist verse is highly formal.[3] She hoped for publication. Weil was also writing in a field dominated by men, at a time when women were not expected to take part in intellectual and artistic life. (William Rees's anthology *The Penguin Book of French Poetry 1820–1950* (1980), for example, offers only three women poets out of a total of fifty-six.) Her work matches the contention of Audre Lorde:

> For women . . . poetry is not a luxury. It is a vital necessity of our existence. It forms the quality of the light within which we predicate our hopes and dreams toward survival and change, first made into language, then into idea, then into more tangible action. (2017: 8)

Now that canons and syllabuses are being revised to include more women writers, Weil demands attention. In a class photograph

---

[3]Valéry was also a major influence on Rainer Maria Rilke, who translated him (Catling 2007: 1091).

of 1926, she stares directly and defiantly at the camera, arms folded, surrounded by men, ready to go her own way. Poetry was not a luxury for her but part of the mindset that made her a philosopher and an activist, and readers must take the poet into account when discussing her significance.

Three early poems

In 1922, while at the Lycée Fénelon in Paris, Weil wrote 'To a Rich Girl' for her friend Suzanne Gauchon (later Suzanne Aron, the wife of Raymond Aron). It angrily addresses 'Clymene', who fails to see the plight of the oppressed from her position of privilege, but it can be interpreted as an expression of self-reproach (following Nevin 1991: 419 n.70), given that justice for the downtrodden and marginalized would be a central concern throughout Weil's life and philosophy.

Weil was born in Paris in 1909 to secular Jewish parents, Bernard and Selma Weil. She had one brother, André, a mathematical genius (see Olsson 2019; Sylvie Weil 2009), who inadvertently caused Weil to feel inferior throughout her life. Her father was a doctor and she always had an uneasy relationship with her bourgeois background, as can be seen in her attitude to comfort. As a schoolteacher, she refused to heat her flat in solidarity with the poor, and at the end of her life in England, she would not eat more than what the citizens of occupied France were, in her opinion, able to eat, which contributed to her death from tuberculosis in 1943 at a time when she was overworked and anxious. The rich girl in the poem is accused of living in a 'greenhouse', where she is 'tranquil and removed from wretched sisters' fate', forgetful of how quickly time will pass. Two groups of these 'wretched sisters' are described: women who work in inhuman conditions in factories and women who work as prostitutes. The poem concludes by telling the rich girl to leave the greenhouse in order to confront the frozen world 'naked and trembling', a phrase that coincidentally occurs in Alan Ginsberg's 1954–5 poem *Howl*, a scream of protest often taken to epitomize the Beat Generation. Weil despised compromise in her own and others' lives and would frequently obey the poem's closing injunction.

Academically brilliant, she studied at two elite Parisian institutions. At the Lycée Henri-IV, she prepared for university entrance, before moving on to a philosophy degree at the École Normale Supérieure in 1928. She then taught philosophy in various schools, finding time to engage in political activity on behalf of both workers and unemployed (to the profound discontent of the authorities), becoming intensely involved in radical causes and producing political journalism and theory (see OL). She left teaching to spend a year working in factories in 1934–5. Like Robyn Penrose, the idealistic lecturer in David

Lodge's novel *Nice Work* (1988), the intellectual was brought face to face with the horrors of industry. However, Weil was no mere observer but a machinist who took on the slavery of 'work at the belt', renouncing 'each slow gesture' that made her 'a queen' and wrecking her already fragile health. She describes her motivation:

> Only when I think that the great Bolshevik leaders proposed to create a free working class and that doubtless none of them – certainly not Trotsky, and I don't think Lenin either – had ever set foot in a factory, so that they hadn't the faintest idea of the real conditions which make servitude or freedom for the workers – well, politics appears to me a sinister farce. (SL 15)

Unlike many intellectuals, she had 'skin in the game', as essayist N. N. Taleb puts it (2018: 184), which is another reason why her works appeal to a wider audience. She would later take on backbreaking work in the fields when resident in Vichy France, labouring for long hours in conditions for which she was physically unsuited, insisting on living in the poorest accommodation and eating very little.

Throughout her life, Weil also showed an interest in the plight of prostitutes, while remaining contemptuous of men who avail themselves of the women who soil 'servile flesh' for a few coins, as she puts it in the poem. To give three examples: in 1937, she disguised herself as a young man and visited a brothel in order to encounter the workers, only to be chased out; in 1940, she was interrogated by the Vichy police on the (justified) suspicion of distributing illegal material for the Resistance and was threatened with being thrown into a cell with the prostitutes, only to reply that she would be happy for a chance to get to know them; in *Venice Saved*, the Courtesan is an interesting character (in contrast to the rather flat figure of Violetta) and Weil sketches the betrayals that have forced the Courtesan into prostitution and given her such a hatred for the Venetians, a hatred that parallels the anger against the rich girl (VS 77–8).

The poem thus implies an author who would rather live out her philosophy than remain in the drawing room or the classroom. Weil's activist attitude has led many readers to see her as a holy figure. Nelson notes that intellectuals call her 'our kind of saint' (2017: 19), while Sylvie Weil records being treated like a relic – a 'saint's tibia' – by devotees of her late aunt (2020: 17–21). It is today possible to buy a Weil icon (available on wood, T-shirt or mug). Rosemary Waugh makes the case, however, that something is lost by such unofficial canonization:

> Given her mysticism, and her powerful connection to the Catholic Church, it may well be tempting to emphasise Weil's Christ-like qualities, but it also feels awkward given her own criticisms of personal fame and individualistic gain . . . being saintly simply makes her less human. (2021: 51)

After all, Weil would never become a Catholic, preferring to remain a Christian outside the institution (LP 3). Palle Yourgrau argues for an alternative categorization:

> she could just as easily be compared with the ancient Hebrew prophets, for whom the smallest human injustice threatens the very foundation of the universe. (2011: 11)

Such a comparison makes better sense and can be applied to the poetry, including this first poem's denunciation of privilege. Regarding Weil as a prophet rather than as a saint also avoids the dangers of hagiography, so that a critical stance towards her thought can be taken. Robert Zaretsky, for example, takes such a stance by arguing that many of the demands that she makes are unreasonable, such as her advocacy of front-line nurses (see later) (2021: 158–60). 'To a Rich Girl' finally also functions as a type of the ultimate prophecy, a memento mori. Beauty will fade and the night of death awaits everyone, which makes it only more important to act now. Even after her move towards Christianity, Weil did not stress the afterlife and saw moral action as necessary in its own right rather than for any reward it might bring.

Weil produced 'Verses Read at the Feast of Saint Charlemagne' as a piece of occasional verse in 1926 when at the Lycée Henri-IV. She showed it to her philosophy teacher Émile-Auguste Chartier, known as Alain, a prominent figure in French philosophy at that time, who exercised a profound and lasting effect on her. Alain introduced her to Plato and taught her to base philosophy on the close reading of primary (rather than secondary) texts. His comment on 'Charlemagne' was brief and to the point: 'We've all written bad poetry when we were young' (see earlier). It is hard to disagree, because 'Charlemagne' is didactic, led by its form and overly discursive, even if technically competent. The poem is nonetheless interesting if read as a poetic investigation into violence.

It was written eight years after the end of the First World War, in which Weil's father had served as a doctor. Weil had adopted a front-line soldier as a penfriend, who visited her and was killed soon afterwards. The poem celebrates the glory of Charlemagne but stresses that peacetime brings its own problems. The martial figure of the Emperor must be consigned to the past in favour of spiritual combat, an image frequently found in religious writings, such as the Bhagavad Gita, the letters of Saint Paul or John Bunyan's *Pilgrim's Progress*, and used by Arthur Rimbaud in *Une saison en enfer*[A Season in Hell], to which Weil refers in a poetic fragment on Rimbaud in her unpublished papers. 'Charlemagne' ends with a vision of how youthful exuberance might be better channelled. The warlord can be replaced with a gentler saint, possibly Saint Genevieve, who will watch over and save the sleeping city, which mirrors the role of Jaffier in *Venice Saved*. Weil, despite her left-wing views and her many criticisms of France, was an advocate of what Zaretsky calls 'compassionate patriotism' (2021: 104) (see NR). She would argue in *The Need for Roots* that we need to be rooted in a country and that we must simultaneously reject unjust State practices such as colonial conquest, which inevitably involves the uprooting of the colonized.[4] The Spanish conspirators in *Venice Saved* are condemned by the play's logic because of their plans to uproot Venetian culture. (They plan to destroy Venice's churches, for example, and to replace them with ones built in Spanish style.) The figure of Charlemagne is important in the poem as a representation of rootedness, even if the point is to move on, just as Weil would argue that there would be a chance for France to experience moral rebirth after the Second World War (see NR).

The young Weil was a pacifist, with her political writings showing the same desire to avoid conflict that can be found in 'Charlemagne'. And yet this follower of the gentle Genevieve was so horrified by the rise of Fascism in Spain that in 1936 she felt driven to serve on the Republican side in an anarchist brigade in the Spanish Civil War. Photographs show her in uniform, carrying a rifle and looking very happy, the ultimately engaged philosopher. She was naturally clumsy – in factory work, she frequently burned and hurt herself – and was quickly forbidden to use weapons. She then seriously injured her leg by stepping

---

[4]Weil's anti-colonialism can be dated to 1930. It is absent from this poem.

into a pan of boiling fat and had to leave the front. Her unit was later annihilated by Nationalist forces and biographers comment that her tendency to speak her mind to superiors would probably have sent her to the firing squad before too long, in any case.

After Spain, Weil denounced atrocities committed by both sides in the conflict. Writing to the right-wing novelist Georges Bernanos, the left-wing philosopher Weil described Republican executions as 'murder'; a young Fascist, executed by Republicans for refusing to change sides, was for her a 'hero' (SL 107–8). Such a view of heroism is far removed from 'Charlemagne', where 'young victors' joyfully desire to follow the Emperor in an unproblematic cause and do not face being shot for their views. Weil, whose political philosophy shows the ability to look past surface phenomena to the harsh realities underneath, deconstructed the Spanish Civil War as a power game between Nazi Germany and Fascist Italy versus Soviet Russia. She would, however, renounce pacifism in 1939 in view of the dangers posed by Nazism, of which she had become especially aware since her extended visit to Berlin in 1932.

Weil sees the problem of violence as fundamental. Communism is inevitably doomed because of the human predilection for violence (OL 62) and the very concept of revolution is empty (OL 53). By the left-wing standards of the time she was a heretic, unafraid to criticize Stalin's Russia. She reads Homer's *Iliad* as a poem of 'force' (IP). Any religion that appeals to violence – which in practice means most religions, including Catholicism – is categorized by her as totalitarian and idolatrous. When in London, working for the French government in exile, she pestered her superiors to be sent to occupied France as an operative or to be allowed to lead a team of front-line nurses who would support fighting men, in a moral reversal of the SS. Both schemes were rejected, to the intense disappointment of the young woman who now desired 'to join the fight and die' like the young men in 'Charlemagne'.

The mention of Durandal and Joyeuse, swords belonging to Roland and Charlemagne, respectively, relates the poem intertextually to the anonymous eleventh-century Old French epic *La Chanson de Roland* [Song of Roland], on which Weil answered questions when taking her baccalaureate in 1924, impressing her oral examiner. The *Chanson* has a stark message. Christians are right and 'pagans' – the Franks' Muslim adversaries – are wrong (1990: 90). 'Charlemagne' recognizes that the heroic age is over but that new ways of heroism can be constructed to move the world on from such crude dichotomies. Weil would come to admire T. E. Lawrence (1888–1935), better known as Lawrence of Arabia, who for her exemplified a new form of heroism. In 1938, she read *The Seven Pillars of Wisdom* (his 1926 account of his role in the Arab revolt against the Ottoman Empire during the First World War) and found in him both military heroism and lucidity of spirit, a 'kind of saint'

(SL 93). Lawrence, the man of letters and of action, was a role model for Weil, who was prepared to risk torture and execution in occupied France.

'Lightning' was written in 1929 and completes this trinity of adolescent verse. It is a visionary lyric that encapsulates an ecological cycle. Clouds part and the world is reborn but inevitably becomes an industrial hell. The poem's imagery forms a creation myth. The narrator calls various aspects of the world into being from 'the pure sky', and phenomena obediently appear: the wind, the city, the sea, the light and the world. These goods are juxtaposed with their antitheses, however, so that the lamp leads to the horror of the mine – Weil once visited a mine and asked to be employed as a miner – and the overall mood is pessimistic. Nature is beautiful, yet our tendency to violence reduces it to a rubbish dump. Weil's insistence that human nature leads to disaster, particularly when people organize themselves in groups, even made her advocate the abolition of political parties (see APP). Some sort of hope is maintained at the conclusion of the poem in the memory of the clear sky that allowed a world to be born at the parting of clouds. The promise of beauty can draw the intellect to a purer realm. Weil would theorize beauty as one 'form of the implicit love of God' (WG 137 ff.), and Jaffier, the protagonist of *Venice Saved*, acts in response to the beauty of the city. (In 'Lightning', the city is also beautiful, like Venice, but falls at last to industrial fumes.)

Weil constructs reality here in terms of opposites, the light and the dark, just as her later philosophy juxtaposes 'gravity' and 'grace' as the powers that, respectively, bring us down or redeem us (see GG 1–4). At a first glance, her approach might seem dualistic, but McCullough is right to argue that the polar opposites in Weil are dialectical, maximized 'in order that they be reconciled in a transcendent harmony' (2014: 214–15). 'Lightning', as its title indicates, places a stress on the light, a trope that is prominent in the later poetry: the final line of *Venice Saved* is 'the rays of day'.

These three early poems are therefore prophetic in two senses. First, they point forward to Weil's activism. Second, in their own right, they challenge the world as human beings have made it: its privileging of rich over poor; its violence; and its environmental degradation. Weil would write no more verse until 1937, when a visit to Italy brought her back to what Gabriella Fiori calls 'the vocation of poetry' (1989: 162).

Six late poems

Weil's later thought turned towards Christianity as a result of three encounters with Catholicism: at a village festival in Portugal in 1935, she concluded that Christianity was a slave religion with which she could identify after her work at the factory belt; in Assisi in 1937, site of the ministry of Saint

Francis, she felt compelled to fall to her knees; while attending the Easter services at the Benedictine Abbey of Solesmes in 1938, she became convinced that Christ had taken possession of her. Some of her later writings can be described as mystical, and many people read Weil for this religious aspect, rather than for her other philosophy. At Solesmes, she also came across George Herbert's poem 'Love (III)' (Herbert 1885: 197–8), in which the narrator speaks with the God who is Love. Herbert's poem enacts the sort of mystical theology that would become central to Weil's thought (see WG 69). Its narrator resists the entreaties of Love, protesting unworthiness, but remains attentive to the divine voice, which persists until the narrator surrenders:

You must sit down, says Love, and taste my meat:
    So I did sit and eat.

Weil became an attentive reader of Herbert's poem, learning it by heart and reciting it as a prayer, which illustrates the importance that verse can have in the form of life of the reader. Poems are recited at weddings and funerals; people write verse when they fall in love; magical spells from around the world are written as poems; popular song lyrics – from Beyoncé to the Beatles – frame the way that millions of people live. Poetry matters, and it mattered to Weil.

Unlike the verse of Herbert, Weil's poems are not overtly Christian. The situation is more like that of the work of

J. R. R. Tolkien, whose imaginary world of Middle Earth is rooted in his Catholicism (see Bernthal 2014), but whose hobbits, for example, do not follow religious practices. Weil similarly writes with a visionary non-dogmatism:

> This attentive and loving gaze, by a shock on the rebound, causes a source of light to flash on the soul which illuminates all aspects of life on this earth. Dogmas lose their virtue as soon as they are affirmed. (LP 30)

Dogmatism was one of the main charges she made against Catholicism. She saw the Church's use of the words 'anathema sit' [Greek/Latin: let them be accursed] against its opponents as an instance of this tendency. For Weil, God has withdrawn from the world, which makes dogmatic pronouncements senseless, and God is similarly absent from the poems. Scholars frequently comment on the – apparently coincidental – similarity between her later thought and the Kabbalistic work of Isaac Luria (1534–72), which postulates an absent God, traces of whose presence can be discerned by correct practice (see Zaretsky 2021: 139–40). The later poems illustrate this similarity.

'Mysticism' is a notoriously difficult term to pin down but can be taken as designating a direct relationship with the ineffable (see Wilson 2018). Weil's mysticism uses the language and insights of Plato, who for her was 'an authentic mystic, perhaps the father of western mysticism' (IC 77), and his ongoing influence on her work shows the continuity in her thinking, which develops but never radically shifts course. She sees mysticism as representing the truth of the world's various religious traditions (LP 29). It is noteworthy how many mystics from different religious traditions have turned to poetry as a way of showing their readers what is beyond words (see Housden 2009), because, as Willis Barnstone argues, mystical poems can bring readers 'closer to the experience of the light than conceptual explanations' (1972: 27). Weil's later poems instantiate her mystical quest, 'staking a claim to that exclusive realm of truth where her brother was resident', as Thomas R. Nevin puts it (1991: 157).

Her return to poetry was triggered by a vacation to Italy in 1937, which included the time in Assisi. (She made a second Italian journey in 1938, when she visited Venice.) Weil wrote that Italy 'reawakened the impulse to write poetry, which I had repressed, for various reasons, since adolescence' (SL 93). It is easy to view Weil as a miserable character – Nelson calls her 'dour' (2017: 2) – but that is to obscure the fact that she could be very open to what life has to offer, be it rugby, tobacco, the novels of Jane Austen or the comic genius of Charlie Chaplin. She enjoyed both reading poetry and writing it. Her accounts of Italy show somebody intoxicated on Italian music, art, opera, sculpture, literature and architecture. She describes visits to restaurants and the cinema with enthusiasm. Italy was under Fascist dictatorship at the time and was pursuing a brutal colonial programme in Africa, but that did not prevent the anti-Fascist and anti-colonialist Weil from seeing value in Italian art and people, a value that she believed would outlast Mussolini's tyranny. As Fiori comments, Italy was for her 'an island of the soul' (1989: 158).

Like Jaffier, Weil responded to the beauty of Italy as something pointing beyond itself. Beauty can draw people to the supernatural even if they have no religious commitment as such:

> The only true beauty which is the real presence of God, is the beauty of the universe. Nothing which is less than the universe is beautiful. (WG 175)

It is a Platonic point of view. Plato's Socrates speaks of the need for the philosopher to ascend to true beauty (*Symposium* 211c) and views artists as counterfeiters because they operate at two removes from the ideal, which is why he would banish them from his ideal state (cf. *Republic* 607b). Weil does not follow Socrates to this conclusion.[5] Finding in Italy beauty in the arts, she was instead moved to write her own literature. For her, the beautiful poem is 'the one which is composed while the attention is kept directed toward inexpressible inspiration, in so far as it is inexpressible' (GG 97). The poetic journey begins with attention and ends in the attempt to communicate what has been seen,

---

[5]For a defence of the arts by a Platonist influenced by Weil, see Murdoch (1997).

a process that parallels Thomas Aquinas's contention that the highest form of life is to pass on to others the things that have been contemplated (ST 3.40.1).

'Prometheus' was written in 1937, as Europe headed towards war. The legendary Titan Prometheus has a distinguished literary pedigree. He is the hero of a seminal Greek tragedy by Aeschylus, which Weil loved, of a poem by Johann Wolfgang von Goethe and of a ballet by Ludwig van Beethoven. Percy Bysshe Shelley wrote a play about him and the alternative title of Mary Shelley's novel *Frankenstein* is *The Modern Prometheus*. For Karl Marx, he was the 'foremost saint and martyr in the philosopher's calendar' (in Prawer 1976: 1). 'Prometheus' is – untypically for Weil's later verse – a narrative poem. She depicts Prometheus as a figure who redeems humanity by the gift of fire rather than as a rebel against divine order. He suffers for humankind in a type of crucifixion, in line with her view that his story is 'the refraction into eternity of the Passion of Christ' (IC 70).[6] One reason that she could never enter the Catholic Church was that she saw such redeemer figures outside Christianity. Christ for her was identical to Dionysus, Krishna, Noah, Odin, Osiris and other

---

[6]Analogously, there is a 1908 sculpture by Auguste Rodin of the crucified Jesus embraced by Mary Magdalene, which has the alternative title 'Prometheus and the Oceanid'. Versions are in the J. Paul Getty Museum, Los Angeles, and the Musée Rodin, Paris.

saviours, as well as to Prometheus, whose body 'twists in vain, under constraint' and whose screams are heard only by the wind.

Weil sent the poem to Valéry, whose verse she admired. That she should write to such a prominent literary figure is itself an indication of her aspirations for her poetry. Nevin argues that she walks in Valéry's 'semantic ambit', following 'his pursuit, with a concession to final impossibility, of what may be pure and absolute within the flood of ordinary impressions and discourse' (1991: 158).[7] In his reply (PVS 9–10), he praises the poem's construction and its firmness, fullness and force. He commends its technical competence and overall strength and notes that there are many successful lines, even if he also finds it too long. Overall, he sees it as too didactic, too instructive and too content to list Prometheus's achievements. There is a rule in creative writing classes: poets must show, not tell; or at least they must tell by showing. Weil breaks the rule here and elsewhere in her poems, but the work after 'Prometheus' is generally less didactic, possibly indicating how she was attentive to Valéry as mentor.

That Weil was drawn to a Greek rather than a Hebrew myth is unsurprising, because she constantly praises Greek thought and culture, discerns intimations of Christianity in Greek literature (see IC) and conversely dismisses most of the Hebrew scriptures for their presentation of a violent God of war,

---

[7]See Chapter 2 for more on Weil and Valéry.

accepting only 'Isaiah, Job, the Song of Solomon, Tobias, part of Ezekiel, part of the Psalms, part of the Books of Wisdom, the beginning of Genesis . . .' (LP 41). This horror of the Hebrew God is found in Gnostic writings, in the teachings of Marcion and in Catharism, all of which are heretical by Catholic standards. For her, the Jewish religion and the Roman state were the two great villains on the stage of world history and the prime corruptors of Christianity (see WG 183).[8]

Prometheus is 'alone, nameless, flesh bound by affliction'. The theme of affliction – French *malheur* – is important to Weil, who defines it as more than unhappiness. It is rather 'an uprooting of life, a more or less attenuated equivalent of death, made irresistibly present to the soul by the attack or immediate apprehension of physical pain' (WG 118). Weil came to know affliction in her own life through factory work and the crippling headaches to which she was prone (and that eventually compelled her to take permanent leave from teaching). She was drawn to Christianity because she viewed it as seeking 'not a supernatural remedy for suffering but a supernatural use for it' (GG 81). Her writings emphasize the crucifixion over the resurrection. Like Jesus, Prometheus offers salvation – Jesus also came to cast fire

---

[8]Many of Weil's readers have been troubled by anti-Semitic remarks in her writings and by her silence about the Holocaust. For a full discussion, see Yourgrau (2011: 117–35).

on the earth (Lk. 12.49) – but the price that he pays is similarly high: a crucifixion in which the reader is invited to share.

'To a Day' was written in 1938. Weil sent a copy to Valéry, who this time did not reply, to her disappointment. She was keen to publish the poem, partly because she had come to feel that the fall of France in 1940 had given it 'a good deal of timeliness' (in Nevin 1991: 159), although it is written to a metaphysical rather than a political agenda. It revisits the ideas of 'Lightning' and shows how daylight serves only to illuminate the necessary destruction of the world. Two lines can be intertextually related to 'To a Rich Girl', again showing continuity in Weil's thought:

From the factories' heavy tumult,
from the markets where flesh is soiled . . .

The rich girl realizes that factories still operate, that flesh is still soiled. She asks if eyes can ever be bathed by light, but the question is not answered here, though it will be at the end of her final poem, 'The Gate'. This poem ends on the image of blind fate, which has decreed that 'this is the last of the days', a fitting description of France in defeat.

'To a Day' is typical of Weil's poetry in that it is framed as an address. Her first two poems are written to people: Clymene in 'To a Rich Girl'; her fellow students in 'Charlemagne'. Other poems invoke lightning, the day, the sea, necessity and the stars, with 'Prometheus' taking a third-person view and 'The Gate' written in the first-person plural. *Venice Saved* ends with an apostrophe of daybreak on the Adriatic by Violetta. There is no use of the lyric 'I' that is so common in French poetry, and the later poems mention no individuals who can be investigated by a biographer. The style of the poems thus mirrors her metaphysical and ethical views: truth is seen as impersonal, a view paralleled in mystical works that have no named author, such as the *Song of Songs,* the Bhagavad Gita and the *Cloud of Unknowing.* Weil, while capable of great affection for family and friends, as can be seen from her letters, was determined to move beyond human relationships, following the Socrates of Plato's *Symposium* (211b). She lived a resolutely asexual life – one of her university teachers dubbed her 'the Red Virgin' – and she would die both exiled and alone.

These later poems can be read through her Platonism. 'To a Day' is an instantiation of how attention can discern the true reality behind appearances. As Nevin argues (1991: 160–1), the parable of the Cave (*Republic* 514) is an important reference point for her poetic writing. In that parable, Socrates describes prisoners who lie shackled in an underground cave lit by a fire, to which they have their backs. They watch shadows cast on the wall, as events take place behind them, and mistake these shadows for reality. Socrates asserts that philosophical activity can allow the prisoners to leave the cave to see the true world in the light of the sun. Weil's poetic voice maintains humility before phenomena, in order to be receptive to the possibility of liberation from the cave:

> I look upon the suspension of judgement with regard to all thoughts whatever they may be without any exception, as constituting the virtue of humility in the domain of the intelligence. (LP 3)

It is poetry of what she calls 'decreation', a paradoxically 'passive activity' (WG 194) that involves the transformation of the self from 'something that belonged to the natural world, into something that belonged to God' (Plant 2007: 41–2).

Weil wrote her final four poems in 1941–2. She had fled Paris with her parents as France fell to Hitler's Germany and lived for two years in the new collaborationist state of Vichy. She spent time in Marseille and labouring in the countryside. In terms of writing, this period was extraordinarily productive.[9] Her thought was crystallizing as a unique blend of the mystical, the philosophical and the political. She developed an interest in Catharism, a Christian Gnostic civilization that flourished between the twelfth and fourteenth centuries in the Languedoc,

---

[9]Most of the work for which she is known was written now, including her *Cahiers* [Notebooks], which form the source for *Gravity and Grace*, a highly influential posthumous anthology compiled by Weil's friend the farmer and philosopher Gustave Thibon, who has been accused of presenting Weil as more Catholic than she was.

before being exterminated by Catholic crusade and inquisition. The Cathars held this world to be a battlefield between a God of light and a God of darkness. Weil saw them as representing an alternative mystical tradition with which she could identify:

> I believe that one and the same thought inhabited all its best minds and was expressed in various forms in the mysteries and the initiatory sects of Egypt, Thrace, Greece, and Persia, and that the works of Plato are the most perfect written expression which we possess of that thought . . . only the Gnostics, Manichaeans and Cathars seem to have kept really faithful to it. (SL 130)

These poems can be read as her own attempts to be faithful to this 'one and the same thought'. They form poetic meditations on four philosophical themes: beauty, necessity, absence and attention. Simone Kotva argues that while it is wrong to describe her as a Gnostic in her beliefs, Weil does adopt a Gnostic *methodology* in her religious philosophy by seeking a hidden truth (2020), and we suggest that the last poems belong to this methodology.[10]

'The Sea' is a direct address to a natural phenomenon, which is personified as 'our sister' and asked to enter into the soul

---

[10]For insightful accounts of Weil and Catharism, see also Barber (2000: 240–4), Plant (2007: 87 ff.) and McCullough (2014: 214–20), who show how views of Weil as a believing Cathar are misguided.

and wash it clean, in what Nevin calls 'a kind of Stoic baptism' (1991: 158).[11] The sea was important to Weil. She was fond of swimming and once went out on a trawler to help the fishermen. It is a constant presence in *Venice Saved*, which begins with the city about to celebrate the anniversary of its marriage to the Adriatic and ends with Violetta greeting the waters' beauty as the festival dawns. Weil in 'The Sea' addresses both natural and supernatural phenomena in a gaze that does not falter. While at ebb, the sea is also chained to eternity. No acquaintance with Weil's philosophy is necessary to appreciate the poem, because it is showing the reader something, weaving metaphysics into an intense depiction of the world. The sea represents both beauty and obedience: it is a 'mirror of obedience', a blended image that we have used as the title for this volume and that shows how for Weil disobedience is not an option, for we must obey *either* gravity *or* grace (cf. WG 128). Like other forms of the love of God, the beauty of the world reveals itself to the one who can contemplate it attentively and see it both as itself, in its particularity, and as a manifestation of divine necessity. In the sea, people behold their fate, but must work out that fate themselves, must work out what they will obey. Through such attention, the mind is cleared and the ego transformed.

---

[11]Weil revered the Stoic thinkers Epictetus and Marcus Aurelius (Zaretsky 2021: 74). See also 'Necessity'.

Humanity is, however, afflicted. People are crushed at the sea's edge and lost within its desert. The poem appeals to the sea to speak 'to those who sink, before they are drowned'. Weil never turns her gaze away from the fact that there are victims of gravity as well as beneficiaries of grace, yet maintains that the sea 'is not less beautiful in our eyes because we know that sometimes ships are wrecked by it', which means that the sea's beauty is constituted by a 'perfect obedience' (WG 129). The sea is thus a fitting symbol of necessity, which is the subject of the next poem.

Weil turns in 'Necessity' to one of the oldest questions in philosophy: Are we free or must we do what is decreed for us (by the stars, by God, by the physical world)? The poem's voice sees humanity as determined, which brings terrible consequences, and yet people must learn to love this state of affairs, must desire to obey 'unto death'. In Weil's thought, the whole of reality, living beings included, follows the laws of necessity, laid down through God's withdrawal. Humanity tends towards gravity, which includes self-affirmation and, paradoxically, the denial of necessity. The effort to lift oneself out of this tendency is at the same time an acceptance of determinism and a heroic denial of natural human evil (as seen in Weil's presentation of the salvific figure of Prometheus). 'Necessity' again shows the essential unity of Weil's thought, here though her continued advocacy of the Stoic *amor fati*

[Latin: love of destiny], found in both 'The Sea' and her early thought (cf. WG 65, OL 81).[12]

For Weil, necessity affects all the natural movements of the soul, with grace being the only exception (GG 1). Again, we must always be obedient to something, as McCullough argues: 'God intervenes universally in every event by withdrawing and allows the world to carry on in accordance with necessity' (2018: 463). Weil was deeply influenced by Jesus's saying that God the Father sends the sun and the rain on the evil and the just (Matt. 5.45; see GG 43). The problem of evil, central to Western philosophy of religion, dissolves. To complain about God allowing evil to exist is to miss the point: 'We have to deserve, by the strength of our love, to suffer constraint' (GG 44). Life will therefore often be pitiless and harsh (Plant 2007: 47). The only perfect figure in the poem is the slow stars (Dargan 1999: 91), and stars are addressed in the next poem.

In 'The Stars', Weil again paints a beautiful but indifferent universe from which God has withdrawn. These are the same stars presiding over the mirror of obedience in 'The Sea' and dancing in 'Necessity'. Stars also connote fate: in 'Charlemagne' the elders wonder 'what fate the stars prophesy' to the 'young silent walkers'. They are unresponsive to human affliction, so all

---

[12]Weil actually took the term *amor fati* from her 'arch adversary' Friedrich Nietzsche, according to Martin Andic (cited in McCullough 2014: 246 n.5).

that humanity can do is to contemplate their 'so pure but bitter light'. The poem can be read as mystical because it uses what *can* be talked about in order to speak about what *cannot*, contradictory as that sounds. De Lussy argues that poetry for Weil represents a privileged mode of access to transcendent realities (in O 802), a view that places Weil alongside mystics who use metaphor as a means of pointing towards the inexpressible, such as John of the Cross, whose erotic poetry acts out God's love for the soul (cf. 1972: 38–41), or Angelus Silesius (Johannes Scheffler), who sees God as the fire within (1986: 39). The stars indicate what lies beyond the stars.

Finally, the waiting is rewarded as astral fire penetrates the heart. Once intelligence becomes silent in order to let love invade the whole soul, then it 'begins once more to exercise itself, it finds it contains more light than before, a greater aptitude for grasping objects, truths that are proper to it' (LP 37). The metaphor of fire in 'The Stars' is the same as used by Angelus Silesius. It is the fire that both Prometheus and Jesus bring to earth. Through this fire, the viewer is transformed, but such mystical renewal comes about through attention, not through any action by the stars.

Weil's final lyric, 'The Gate', is written in the voice of somebody standing in front of a mysterious gate, waiting for it to be opened. The poem is about attention itself, her major mystical and ethical theme. Attention involves allowing the object of attention to be, without distorting or possessing, and responding only to the call of necessity, rather than to will or desire. This ethical aspect depends in turn on Weil's mysticism, where attention is the faculty that reveals the reality that we do not normally access, for we labour behind a veil of illusion. The ambiguity between 'deeper' and 'higher' levels of reality is central to the poem. The gate offers both the illusion of consolation and the presence of a void which, if accepted, sheds a different light on the world we inhabit. The poem is emblematic of Weil herself, who is often described as a liminal figure and who was facing a threshold in her own life at this time, as conditions in Vichy worsened for Jews and the Weils were forced to consider emigration. It is also reminiscent of a story in Franz Kafka's posthumous 1925 novel *The Trial*, told by a priest to Josef K., about a man from the country who waits for years in front of the gate to the law, seeing a radiance only as he dies, when the gate is closed forever (1994: 166–7). Kafka's image is in turn taken up by J. M. Coetzee in 'At the Gate', the penultimate chapter of his novel *Elizabeth Costello* (2003). In Weil's poem, there is no gatekeeper: the waiting is what is being described. De Lussy argues that the poem both depicts the gateway to the transcendent and becomes itself a gateway for the reader (in O 805 n.1).

'The Gate' juxtaposes contradictions. Weil sees this world as 'the closed door . . . a barrier' that was 'at the same time a way through' (GG 145), and this dual role is played by the gate, which offers 'neither orchards nor flowers' but 'the immense space of the void and of the light'. Unlike many philosophers, she could maintain more than one possibility in her thinking, as Zaretsky notes: 'Reflecting upon a problem, rather than solving it, was Weil's goal' (2021: 43).[13] For Weil, the ability to contemplate contradiction – which is inherent in human existence – is the essence of philosophy (RCV 108), which means that transcendent truth, normally unavailable to the intellect, can be accessed by holding incompatible truths in view (OL 150).[14] Poetry is the perfect vehicle for presenting aspects that are incompatible with each other, because its metaphors do not demand a logical working out. As Jeremy Noel-Tod argues, poetry has a tendency 'to stimulate the metaphorical movement of the mind' (2019: xxxi), and such metaphorical movement is capable of holding contradictions. Shakespeare's audience, for example, can see Juliet as the sun, even though on the literal level Romeo's astronomy is faulty when he uses this image in *Romeo and Juliet* (2015, Act 2 Scene 2). It is metaphorically possible for Weil to see a gate as a barrier and as a way through at the same time and to explore this contradiction over twenty lines. Her approach is that of the two birds she cites from one of the

---

[13]She adopted this method as a teacher, which meant that her students, while enjoying their classes, did not do well in examinations.

[14]There is a parallel with the mystical writing of Pseudo-Dionysius the Areopagite (late fifth to early sixth century), who advocates holding contradictory views about God's existence in order to make the mind receptive to the divine reality (1987: 136).

Upanishads, who sit on a branch, one eating the fruit and one looking at it, with Weil interpreting them as the two parts of the soul (WG 166).[15]

We have stressed that we are not making any claim that Weil is a great poet, but it seems to us that in this final text she has produced something of genuine poetic interest, coming close to what she says about beautiful poetry:

> In the case of a really beautiful poem the only answer is that the word is there because it is suitable that it should be. The proof of this suitability is that it is there and that the poem is beautiful. The poem is beautiful, that is to say that the reader does not wish it other than it is.
>
> It is in this way that art imitates the beauty of the world. (WG 176)

'The Gate' shows and does not tell, in line with Valéry's advice. It leaves work for the reader to do, without offering explication. At the end, as in Kafka, there is an encounter with light that bathes the eyes, an image also reminiscent of the final line of 'The Sea'.

---

[15]For Mary Midgley, poems 'can show up contradictions and connections we had not noticed', sending the reader back to the messiness of life, which makes it a valuable tool for the metaphysician (in Mac Cumhaill and Wiseman 2022: 264).

Saving Venice

In 1940, Weil began work on her tragedy *Venice Saved*. It is possible to interpret its plot against the events unfolding in Europe. The Spanish mercenaries menacing Venice in 1618 mirror the German forces that first threatened and then crushed France (see Fiori 1989: 187). Weil's death in 1943 prevented her from finishing the play, but she did write its concluding scenes and left notes for unwritten ones, so that it can be read as a unity and has been performed (in French and in English translation) and filmed (in Italian translation). As with the poems, *Venice Saved* was important to her and the subject of extensive revisions. She enjoyed live drama and lamented that she did not have more existences so that she could devote one of them to the theatre (SL 91). Her wish was that her projected collection of poems should include two extracts from the play: Violetta's song to the sea, preceded by Jaffier's final speech (SL 168).[16]

Venice Saved tells of the pity that Jaffier experiences for Venice's beauty. For Weil, cities 'surround the life of their inhabitants with poetry' (WG 180–1). She believed that she was the first person treating the conspiracy to realize the nobility of the motive that leads Jaffier to denounce the plot against the city (Pétrement 1976: 365) and she set out to dramatize her insight with the same

---

[16]We include Jaffier's final three speeches.

respect for tradition that marks her lyrics, employing a stagecraft that is a world away from the experimental work of, say, her contemporary Samuel Beckett. Very little happens on stage and the protagonist's decisive act of betrayal takes place between the second and third acts. The overall statuesque effect is reminiscent of Jean Racine. Even the genre – Weil defines *Venice Saved* as a 'tragedy' on its title page – looks backwards rather than forwards, although the spin taken on tragedy is highly original, given that the play ends with the saving of Venice and the triumphant speech of Violetta (see later). The tragic movement is internal, rooted in Jaffier's affliction.

Much of the play is in formal verse, a radical choice in the modernist era.[17] The use of poetry allows Weil to foreground the play's spiritual themes by saving prose for more mundane speeches, and it also makes demands on the reader, calling for attention in a way that prose does not. *Venice Saved* is a work of declamation rather than action: what happens, happens in the poetry. Her notes on the play show how carefully she designed the verse:

> *This act, like the preceding one, is written for the most part in unrhymed verse of 14 syllables. The Mercenaries speak in prose; Violetta in unrhymed verse of 11 syllables (5-6); Jaffier*

---

[17]There are modernist parallels, however, such as the verse dramas of T. S. Eliot.

replies in unrhymed verse of 13 syllables (5-4-4). Or in 11 as
well? Or Violetta in 13? Or 12 (4-4-4)? Other exceptions?
(VS 88)

Such poetic differentiation foregrounds the intellectual drama.
The concluding address by Violetta, for example, contrasts
in its serene quatrains with the tortured verse of Jaffier's
final speeches.

Jaffier's fate is tragic because he betrays the conspiracy to
the Venetian authorities on the understanding that he and
his friends will be spared; but he is in turn betrayed when his
comrades are arrested, tortured and executed, including his
beloved best friend Pierre. Weil sees friendship as another form
of the implicit love of God (WG 200 ff.) and Jaffier loses this
grace. He calls himself 'malheureux', an 'afflicted man' (PVS
114/VS 100), so that Nevin argues that he is Prometheus, an
object 'so abominated that the earth itself, so his enemies hope,
will be loath to sustain him' (1991: 171), thus closing another
poetic circle in Weil's opus. Jaffier's acceptance of suffering for
performing a just act, 'filial piety for the city of the world' (WG
175), also makes him like Jesus, and like the Jesus of the Passion
he is surrounded by mockery. He must contemplate what is
too terrible to contemplate, the loss of his friends due to his
own action:

My friends will die, all betrayed by me.

The poetry circles around this dilemma. He faces insanity for performing a moral action and his final speeches vocalize a descent into madness. Although he has saved Venice, there will be no dawn where he will go, 'nor any city', such is the depth of his affliction. Unlike Violetta, he cannot stand to behold the day. Fiori argues that it is possible to go one step further in a reading of Jaffier:

> Jaffier, who symbolizes the opposition of the principle of weakness to the dictation of force which has always dominated history, prefigures with his madness a project that Simone was bringing to maturity, of equal opposition. She is Jaffier. (1989: 188)

To see Jaffier as Weil's self-portrait is to be given an insight into the affliction that she bore at the end of her life, similarly 'torn about by pain' – by violent headaches, exile and the frustration of not being able to act for France as the world fell apart. The rich girl freezes.

Another rich girl, Violetta, daughter of the Secretary of the Council of Ten, enters the empty stage after the action is over. The conspiracy has been defeated, the city has been saved and the mercenaries executed. Jaffier, though pardoned, has gone to face his death by joining in what remains of the conspiracy. He has perished so that the beauty of Venice, symbolized by Violetta, can be preserved. She now greets the day in triumph, on the festival marking the anniversary of the city's marriage to the sea, to which she has been looking forward throughout the play. She has been attracted to Jaffier and impressed by these chivalrous strangers, unaware of the horrific plans that some of them were making for her. She is similarly unaware of their horrific fate, which lends an ironic framework to her lines, but the speech still encapsulates a Platonic vision, spoken by one who has left the cave to behold the sun of goodness. Even if the cost is terrible, beauty can still save us: the rays of day are lovely on this sea on this day. The imagery of light meeting water at daybreak intertextually revisits three of the later poems: 'To a Day', 'The Sea' and 'The Stars'. Violetta's exit from the cave into sunlight makes a fitting conclusion to Weil's poetic work.

Violetta is also *rooted* in her 'city and its thousand canals'. Weil, in contrast, was now to uproot herself. In 1942, she and her parents left Vichy and crossed the sea first to North Africa and then to New York. Later that year she sailed alone for Britain to work in administration for the Free France Movement in London. When her requests for direct action in occupied territory were refused, she came to regret choosing what she now saw as safety, writing that leaving Vichy was an 'act of desertion' that was 'like tearing up my roots' (SL 144). She addressed the issues that would face a French government after the war and produced the work known as *The Need for Roots*, while weakening herself by overwork and lack of food. She finally resigned from the Free France Movement. Some commentators have thought that the mystic was now disillusioned with politics as a way of solving problems, although even in 1943 she was insistent that mysticism (from all traditions) necessarily leads to morality (OL 151).

In April 1943, Weil was admitted to hospital in London with tuberculosis and was transferred to the Grosvenor Sanatorium in Ashford, where she died on 24 August. Her death was recorded as suicide 'by refusing to eat when the balance of her mind was disturbed'. It is possible that some form of baptism was administered to her. She practised attention to the end by carrying on her study of Sanskrit, reading the Bhagavad Gita in the original, 'those marvellous words, words with such a Christian sound' (WG 70). She was buried in Ashford. The Catholic priest who was to preside at the funeral missed his train, so one of Weil's friends had to say the prayers, which Stephen Plant calls 'an ironic and final twist' to her time on the margins of the Church (2007: 20).

What remains is the work, which has made her one of the twentieth century's unforgettable figures. Albert Camus wrote to Weil's mother in 1951 that Weil was the only great spirit of their time (in O 91). Her poetry and her verse play demand to be read alongside her theoretical writings, because, as Bryan Magee argues, 'poetry is the continuation of philosophy by other means' (2021: 57) – how different the means are, we shall see in the next chapter.

Weil's prophetic voice makes itself heard after her death. With Camus, she joins a tradition of French thinkers who have produced both philosophy and literature, including Simone de Beauvoir, Denis Diderot, Jean-Paul Sartre, Jean-Jacques Rousseau and Voltaire. In 1935, while labouring in a factory, she had written:

> Perhaps later on I shall find the right words, but at present it seems to me that I should need a new language to convey what needs to be said. (SL 6)

In poetry, she found that language.

2

Simone Weil and literature

On eating and reading

Simone Weil was a voracious reader, a metaphor she employed herself: 'I only read what I am hungry for at the moment when I have an appetite for it, and then I do not read, I eat' (WG 69). This declaration may sound surprising, given that elsewhere she rejects the image of eating, which she saw as a 'consumption' of a reality that we should, instead, contemplate:

> It may be that vice, depravity, and crime are nearly always, or even perhaps always, in their essence, attempts to eat beauty, to eat what we should only look at. Eve began it. If she caused humanity to be lost by eating the fruit, the opposite attitude, looking at the fruit without eating it, should be what is required to save it. (WG 166)

And then she quotes a famous image from an Upanishad: 'two birds are on the branch of a tree. One eats the fruit, the other looks at it', commenting: 'These two birds are the two parts of our soul' (WG 166).

These references illustrate two important and related themes in Weil's thinking. One is that of respect for reality, manifested in attention and in an acknowledgement of the impossibility for us to change or dominate a world that, for her, is governed by necessity. The other, more implicit than explicit in what we have just quoted, is Weil's idea that truth can be found anywhere and is indeed found in very different cultures, languages and eras. Weil the reader discovered profound and essential truths in Plato and Sophocles, in the Upanishads and the Bhagavad Gita, and in Descartes and Kant.

As she wrote in 'Some Reflections around the Concept of Value' in relation to philosophical truth, there is only one true philosophical tradition, 'one, eternal, and not susceptible of progress'. This tradition, she writes, is as old as humanity itself:

Plato is the most perfect representative of this tradition; the Bhagavad Gita is similarly inspired, and one should find easily Egyptian and Chinese texts named alongside them. In Europe, in modern times, it is necessary to cite Descartes and Kant; among recent thinkers, Lagneau and Alain in France, Husserl in Germany. (RCV 110)

This great openness of Weil, her curiosity and desire to seek expressions of truth in many cultures and languages, can explain her hunger for reading and also her willingness to learn other languages. She writes in a letter to Déodat Roché of 21 February 1941:

> For me, in any case, nothing equals the original texts, naked and without commentaries. They alone give me the kind of contact with what I desire to know. I do not mind if I only understand them partially. Only later do I have recourse to studies and commentaries, if there are some that I trust; then I return to the texts. (*Cahiers Simone Weil* 25/2: 143, quoted in Cabaud Meaney 2007: 14)

Her knowledge of ancient Greek is visible from her early years, for instance, in the story of 'The Fairies of the Fire', written at the age of eleven, where the characters are named using Greek words; she also read the New Testament in Greek; and her essay on the *Iliad* offers quotations that she translated herself into French. Weil was also perfectly happy to learn languages as far from her native French as Sanskrit so that she could read the texts and draw in their original inspiration. The desire to learn Sanskrit arose after reading the Bhagavad Gita in the spring of 1940, a text which was to have a lasting influence on her and where she found 'marvellous words, words with such a Christian sound, put into the mouth of an incarnation of God' (WG 70).

Besides finding connections with Christianity, the Indian text made salient for her the idea of 'passive activity', of which she says that it is 'the highest of all' and 'perfectly described' not only in the Bhagavad Gita but also in Lao-Tse and is reminiscent of the harmony of the Pythagoreans (WG 194). All of this will make it unsurprising that in her own literary endeavours, we can see reverberations of Weil's vast reading, spiritual, philosophical and literary.

Marie Cabaud Meaney offers a helpful list of some literary authors that are mentioned by Weil in her essays, notebooks or letters. It is not short. We find Homer, Sophocles, Aeschylus, but also Euripides, Sappho, Virgil; Villon, Marlowe, Shakespeare, Cervantes, Molière, Racine, Scève, d'Aubigné, de Viau, Lamartine, Vigny, Mallarmé; Rabelais, Montaigne, La Boétie, Descartes, Retz, the authors of Port-Royal, Molière, Montesquieu, Rousseau; Goethe, Rimbaud, Anouilh, Buck, Proust, del Vasto, Wilde, Tolstoy, Dostoevsky, Stendhal, Balzac, Hugo, Verlaine, Baudelaire, Romains, Mauriac, Claudel; Dante, Donne, Michelangelo, Francis of Assisi, Brooke, Valéry – and more (see Cabaud Meaney 2007: 23–6).

It seems, then, fair to say that Weil 'devoured' texts. How can we square this affirmation, made using this particular metaphor, with her own rejection of such a grasping attitude, not so much or only in relation to reading, but to reality itself? Let's return to the quotation that opened this section, and add more context:

I had never read any mystical works because I had never felt any call to read them. In reading as in other things I have always striven to practice obedience. There is nothing more favourable to intellectual progress, for as far as possible I only read what I am hungry for at the moment when I have an appetite for it, and then I do not read, I eat. (WG 69)

The first two sentences of this passage introduce another key idea, that of 'obedience'. If we relate it to Weil's statement on reading that follows, we can derive a very different meaning of 'eating' from the one that is expressed by Weil in relation to the birds in the Upanishad or to Eve in the Hebrew scriptures. Obedience, for Weil, is the result of attention, when reality itself reveals to us what we should do – and then we have no choice. It is the willingness to act not out of our own selves and wills but out of a response to what we see when we have abandoned such personal self and will. The eating that results from obedience cannot, then, be an attempt to deny the independent reality of its object, as we do when we are pulled by gravity, but another way of paying passionate attention to it. 'Eating' a text becomes in this context a way not of possessing it – how could we ever possess the *Iliad* or *Antigone*? – but a way of incorporating its inspiration into oneself. The text remains unchanged. Our understanding of the text, too, is not distorted by our wishes or personality. It is the text that possesses us, not the other way around.

The experience of being possessed by a literary text was, indeed, a powerful one for Weil. As we mentioned in Chapter 1, it was while reading George Herbert's poem 'Love' that she felt vividly the presence of Christ. After discovering Herbert's poetry, together with the work of other metaphysical poets, through a 'young English Catholic' in Solesmes in 1938, she would recite 'Love' to herself many times, especially during her frequent painful attacks of migraine. And 'It was during one of these recitations that . . . Christ himself came down and took possession of me' (WG 69).

The poem 'possessed' Weil, or rather, in her more exact words, through the poem Christ possessed her. This is an inversion of the acquisitiveness of human nature, bound by gravity, which seeks to 'eat' in the wrong way, by possessing reality in thought (projecting one's desires, being blind to what is there) or deed (as the Spanish tried to do in *Venice Saved*). Yet in a very different sense Weil 'ate' the poem, insofar as she allowed it to penetrate her soul and act upon her, through an attentive reading which was *obedient* to the text. Strikingly, the last word of the poem is 'eat'.[1] And the eating that occurs in the poem, in response to Love's request, is itself an act of obedience.

The immense importance of Herbert's poem to Weil is evidenced by the fact that she shared it a number of times in

---

[1] See also Cabaud Meaney (2007: 214).

her letters to people who were close to her: in a letter to Father Joseph-Marie Perrin in May 1942, which is the text that we know as 'Spiritual Autobiography' collected in *Waiting for God*; in a letter to her brother André, who was then in prison (Allen 1985: 17); and in a letter to Joë Bousquet, a poet and a veteran of the First World War, in response to his interest in her mystical experience (SL 142).

Through Herbert's poem, Weil directly experienced the great spiritual potential of literature and the capacity of poetry to bring about spiritual transformation and even, for her, a mystical experience. In the letter to Perrin she writes that 'I used to think I was merely reciting it ["Love"] as a beautiful poem, but without my knowing it the recitation had the virtue of a prayer' (WG 68–9). This thought may seem to clash with her idea, expressed only a few pages later in relation to the 'marvellous words' of the Bhagavad Gita, that 'we owe an allegiance to religious truth which is quite different from the admiration we accord to a beautiful poem; it is something far more categorical' (WG 70). But 'Love' (together with a few other literary texts) was for Weil more than a 'beautiful poem', if that is understood as something merely aesthetically pleasing. It was an object of insight or a 'gate' to a higher experience, using the imagery of one of Weil's own poems offered in this book, 'La porte'/'The Gate'. Religious truths and beautiful poems, it turns out, are not at odds. Sometimes, in fact, one is needed to access the other; sometimes they are not even separate.

Poetry, then, presented itself to Weil as something that can appeal to more than the intellect. That was necessary, for Weil saw the intellect as inadequate, on its own, to give us access to fundamental truths. As Diogenes Allen writes, 'Herbert is not merely giving expression to convictions, he is inviting people to *experience* the reality of God's love and in that experience to attain conviction or to deepen conviction. That is precisely what happened to Weil. A poem opened her to an experience which convinced her of the reality of God' (1985: 32; emphasis added).

Yet Weil's intellect was not easily put aside. That's why we can see the poem as a starting point of a longer journey for her. As Allen's essay on Weil as a reader of Herbert concludes, while the presence of 'supernatural good' in the poem 'won her love',

it only half convinced her intellect. It took more visitations and a structure of thought concerning nature's necessity and nature's beauty before she became fully convinced. An experience, even one as powerful as she had, was not sufficient. It had to be connected to other levels of experience and reasoning to give full conviction. Nonetheless, it was a poem which uses the imagination that enabled Weil to break through to a domain above the intellect. (Allen 1985: 34)

As a philosopher, as well as mystic and poet, Weil needed both intellect and experience to be convinced. Yet without the deep experience of love, it is likely that her intellectual path would have been very different and much less rich.

Philosophy and the poetic word

When it comes to Weil's reading of poetry, the most influential contemporary voice for her was doubtless that of Paul Valéry, who inspired her own poetry, with whom, as we have seen, she had a brief correspondence, and whose name appears frequently in her writings and notebooks. Valéry's ideas are also helpful in further understanding the transformative power of poetry for Weil, in her thought and in her own experience. In a lecture delivered at Oxford University in 1939, Valéry argues that the poetic word is different from the ordinary word because it does not have a mostly instrumental function, but it retains salience as an object in itself (Valéry 1954). The ideas developed around the non-instrumental value of poetry are helpful both in understanding the impact of poetry, such as it had on Weil, and in furthering Weil's own ideas on the necessity to move beyond instrumental or goal-oriented thinking and towards the realm of absolute value.

According to Valéry, the poetic word is special because it exhibits a unity with its meaning, being not a means or vessel but an occasion for experience that has no other aim but rather contains its own value. Finally, the poetic word, as a persistent object of attention, evokes a desire that is never satisfied, unlike prose, which extinguishes desire once its goal is achieved (1954: 225). All this, for Valéry, endows it with a 'transformative' potential. The poet, for this reason, possesses a 'spiritual energy of a very special kind' (1954: 229) and 'undergoes a hidden transformation' (1954: 222), in the presence of a word whose meaning goes beyond both the creator and the reader of poetry. Poetry, then, is the transformation of the individual in the presence of words that carry with them a fragment of reality whose significance can neither be exhausted nor specified in any other way.

In these fragments of Valéry's theory of poetry, we see several key elements that Weil sought to bring about in her literary work and which are central to her philosophy too: the aim for total transformation, the experience of absolute value and the necessity of attention and detachment to achieve them. These ideas find a special theoretical articulation in Weil's essay 'Some Reflections around the Concept of Value: On Valéry's Claim that Philosophy Is Poetry', drafted in 1941 and written in response to another lecture by Valéry, delivered in 1937, the first of a series of inaugural addresses as the chair of poetics at the Collège de France – a lecture Weil did not attend but of which she obtained the notes published by a listener in the journal *Yggdrasil*.

Weil writes that the task of philosophy is to reflect on values, and values are unconditional. Yet the human mind does not operate on the level of the unconditional. At the same time, she claims, our minds are always oriented towards value, and they cannot but be so. So philosophy discloses a contradiction, but one that is essential and inescapable. The aim, for Weil, is not to try and resolve the contradiction (which cannot be done) but to expose it and hold it. Very few philosophers, according to her, were able to do so and are therefore worthy of the name.

The task of philosophical thought for Weil, then, is to remain in a state of tension, holding contradictions. This is true of the poetic word too. It is even more explicitly true of tragedy, which in Weil's view dramatizes a tension not just between two conflicting desires or worldviews but two different orders of reality. Such is the tension between the instrumental and the absolute. And such, therefore, is the human condition. Instead of escaping the tension, we must be able to attend to it.

To use Weil's imagery once again, we are always 'at the gate', and true philosophy as well as great literature is able to show us this condition without trying to escape it. Learning to contemplate contradiction is indeed a transformation, not from one state to a different one, but from blindness about our own state to heightened vision. These thoughts also help us understand Valéry's idea of poetic transformation, Jaffier's transformation in *Venice Saved* and Weil's own transformation thanks to Herbert's poem. Such transformation, finally, also requires the attentive detachment that we have seen in relation to the ambiguous metaphor of eating in the previous part of this chapter. Like the attentive 'consumption' of poetry and like the right attitude towards beauty, so

> reflection supposes a transformation in the orientation of the soul that we call detachment. It has for its object establishing an order in the hierarchy of values, thus again a new orientation of the soul. Detachment is a renunciation of all possible ends without exception, a renunciation that puts a void in the place of the future just as the imminent approach of death does. (RCV 109)

Weil's own view of language develops throughout her life, from a more youthful faith in its capacity to order and control (see LOP) to a focus on its capacity to deceive and act as instrument of force when war was looming (see PW), to reflections on the poetic word, silence and contradiction. The last phase, in particular, resonates with Valéry's elevation of the poetic word, showing why she tried to express some of her ideas in poetic form and why she attached so much importance to her literary endeavours.

Weil's ideas about language – helpfully explored by J. P. Little in a rich essay (1996) – show that there is also something about the poetic word that philosophy, when expressed as discursive thought, cannot achieve. Partly, that has to do with poetry's capacity to express contradictions within not just a thought but a line, even a single word. More clearly, it has to do with poetry's capacity to disrupt the linear order of time which binds us. As Little writes, 'Lines of poetry create a new time for the reader. . . . It is effectively a way of escaping from linear time, that time which is for Simone Weil the supreme form of necessity' (1996: 49).

Finally and most importantly, Little argues, poetry's distinctiveness is linked with its closeness to silence: if language, as Weil holds, is still a human and natural phenomenon, we cannot expect a perfect unity of word and truth, despite aiming at it. The best poetry, the poetry that is beautiful in Weil's sense, holds this contradiction too within itself, pointing at the same time at the silence that surrounds it. Again with reference to Valéry, Weil writes in her notes to *Venice Saved*, as we have seen: 'a poem emerges from silence, returns to silence' (VS 57). Silence is the space that we need to allow, the inner emptiness that comes with attention. 'To wait [in silence and patience] is to express in action passivity of thought' (FLN 101, quoted in Little 1996: 48).

The silence that the poetic word brings out and the poetic word's being outside of linear time are not an abdication from expression but the only way of lifting us up above the limitations inherent in language, towards something higher. They are, to use Weil's metaphor about contradictions, a ladder,

or again a gate. Once we are there, as readers of poetry, the only
thing to do is *wait*.

Original readings

When talking about Weil as a reader, it is important to mention
the great significance that the very concept of 'reading' had for
her. Besides the readings of literary, philosophical, spiritual and
scientific texts, there is another form of reading that can be more
immediate and is omnipresent. That is the 'reading' of reality,
whenever we encounter it, and that comes, for Weil, with – not
after – perception. In 'Essay on the Concept of Reading', Weil
opens with these words:

> We shall attempt to define a concept that has not yet found a
> suitable name, but for which the name 'reading' may be the
> best one. For there is a mystery in reading, a mystery that,
> if we contemplate it, may well help us, not to explain, but to
> grab hold of other mysteries in human life. (LPW 21)

Just as, when we read a text, it is not the sensation from the
marks on the page that produces an effect on us, but the
meaning that we read in those marks, so other experiences
too are caused and defined not by the sensations alone, but the
meanings we read into them. Yet we experience the meanings

as already *there*, entering us from the outside. This is, as Weil acknowledges, a contradiction, once again not one we should smooth over, but rather learn from. We *read* love and hate in the faces of others, as if love and hate were just there. Weil draws important ethical and political implications from these observations:

> In the same way, during peacetime, the idea of causing the death of a human being comes from the inside, it isn't read in the appearances – one reads, on the contrary, in the appearances the prohibition of killing. But in a civil war, put somebody in contact with a certain category of human beings and the idea of sparing a life is weak, coming from the inside. There is no transition possible in going from one state to the other; the passage happens as by the pulling of a trigger. Each reading, when it is current, appears as the only real, only possible way to look at things; the other one seems purely imaginary. (LPW 25)

The great question, then, for our lives generally, is how these readings are generated and transformed. Weil asks: Is one reading truer than another? How do we move from one to the other? There is no straightforward answer that she offers. But in reading texts, as in reading reality, we can at least take from Weil the reminder to try and be attentive, which means avoiding any unnecessary imposition of meaning, an imposition that, as Weil shows, is nonetheless inevitable.

In the 'Essay on the Concept of Reading', Weil, as is characteristic of her, takes the idea of reading and applies it to a context that, while familiar, is then shown in a new light. The same can be said of her own readings, in the more literal sense, of well-known literary texts, such as classical tragedies, or the striking essay on the *Iliad*. Never interested in being widely appealing, Weil's overall view of literature is far from what was prevalent in the modernist era in which she lived, and even further from postmodern developments. Weil was not of her time, insofar as what interested her was the timeless. Such timelessness is connected with Weil's interest in what art can tell us about spiritual truths. This search led her, as Katherine T. Brueck writes, to develop a distinctive reading of literature, 'in opposition to a chorus of modernist thinkers who view the interrelation of literature and religion from a philosophical or an anthropological point of view' (Brueck 1995: 14). And more specifically, it led her to develop a distinctive reading of tragedies. As Brueck notes:

The majority of contemporary writers on tragedy, like Aristotle himself, secularize tragedy, thereby ignoring or, at best, marginalizing a central element of tragic experience: the supernatural. Simone Weil, contrarily, suggests that major tragedies in the classical tradition presuppose a fragile but authentic link between suffering innocence and an apprehension of the transcendent. (1995: 3)

The apprehension of the transcendent is visible in Weil's reading of *Antigone*, for instance, as well as in Weil's own tragedy (see VS 23 ff.). Unlike other commentators, who saw two kinds of morality as giving rise to the conflict of the tragedy, Weil read *Antigone* as displaying the infinite distance between natural, human morality and supernatural good, represented, respectively, by Creon and Antigone. These reflections were put into an essay published by the workers' periodical *Entre Nous* in 1936. Also typical of Weil is the intensely social and practical intent behind her interpretations of literary texts. 'For other social classes', she writes in 'Prerequisite to Dignity of Labour', 'poetry is a luxury but the people need poetry as they need bread' (SWA 268).

Weil's reading of the *Iliad*, too, is both distinctive and practical (see IP). In the *Iliad*, Weil finds the manifestation of 'force', the same phenomenon that was plaguing Europe at the time. (The essay appeared in two parts in 1940 and 1941.) To exercise force is a human tendency that is inescapable except through grace, and which turns, in Weil's definition, those subject to it into mere things. To use Weil's earlier reflections, those who have the capacity to use force read nothing into their objects other than an opportunity to use and to destroy. Thus force manifests itself in a war that has no real purpose, according to Weil, and that's exactly why it continues without resolution.

In these brief mentions of Weil's readings of great literary works, we can see an original mind extracting significant and useful lessons that were meant to have both a timeless and a contemporary relevance. In her own literary work, too, Weil tried to offer something similarly timeless and hence timely, by using the poetic word, with the hope of showing up the gravity of the human condition in a truer light, and hence to be transformed by that contemplation.

The translator

Weil's sensitivity to words and their (personal, cultural, political and spiritual) power is evident not only in her own writing, literary or philosophical, but also in her translations. In a letter from London to her parents (who were by now safe in New York) of 9 June 1943, Weil juxtaposes the bistro and the pub (a word that she keeps in English; English words pepper her final letters) to explain differences between England and France:

> Did I ever tell you that a pub and a bistro, side by side, would show more eloquently than many big volumes the difference between the two peoples – their history, their temperament, and the way the social question presents itself for each of them? (SL 189)

She goes into detail about how a British pub of the period was typically divided into public bar and saloon along class lines, with the saloon being more like the French bistro. It is written by somebody who is alive to the difference and similarity that are everywhere in translation.

Interest in the links between translation and philosophy continues to grow. Translation scholars investigate the translation of philosophy and turn to philosophy to support their ideas, while philosophers investigate the theory and practice of translation (Pym 2007; Rawling and Wilson 2019). The voice of Weil as a blend of the philosopher, the translator and the poet can be introduced to this debate. Weil did not write about translation at any length, unlike some twentieth-century philosophers, such as Jacques Derrida or Martin Heidegger, nor was she a philosopher of language, like Ludwig Wittgenstein (see the relevant chapters in Rawling and Wilson 2019); but she did make remarks about translation that are of interest. Even if there is no theory of translation to be extracted from Weil's work, it offers a new voice that is worth hearing. It is salutary and part of a process of recovery to introduce a woman philosopher into an arena dominated by statements made by men (see Shread 2019: 324), but our contention is that Weil should be investigated because of the originality of what she has to say, rather than merely to redress an imbalance.

Philosophizing about translation begins when somebody realizes that rendering a text is never a straightforward conversion from one language to another (Crane 2015: 8). The collection of Weil's letters and essays known in French as *Attente de Dieu* has been translated into English as *Waiting for God*, *Waiting on God* and *Awaiting God*. What is going on? What does this single example have to say about the frequently used notion of 'equivalence'? More generally, what can Weil tell us about translation? And what can translation tell us about Weil?

Weil herself was multilingual. Besides Classical and Hellenistic Greek and Sanskrit, she learned English, German, Italian and Latin. Her reading in both French and world literature was vast, as we stressed earlier, and the foreignness of texts mattered to her. She prayed the Lord's Prayer in Greek and in the letter cited earlier, she describes with enthusiasm what it feels like to be studying Sanskrit again: 'How it does one good, the language of Krishna!' (SL 188). Her view that too much truth lay outside the Catholic Church for her ever to join it through baptism was mirrored in her engagement with languages and literatures other than French. The letter ends with the English expression 'Fondest love' and there is a reference to Samuel Butler's novel *Erewhon* in the postscript (SL 188).

Translation can be viewed as a form of close reading. It is trivially true that nobody can translate a text that they have not read, but translation demands a different *sort* of reading from reading for pleasure or for information. Clive Scott argues that the translator who fails to integrate their reading into a translation is betraying their 'value and destiny as a reader'

(2008: 18), while Michel Deguy goes as far as to describe his French translation of a Seamus Heaney poem as a reading of that text – 'Pylos: Poème lu par Michel Deguy' ['Pylos: Poem read by Michel Deguy'] (2008) – and Lydia Davis argues that one of the pleasures of translation consists in seeing 'how a particular work of literature is put together' (2021: 20). Translation can be a way of understanding a source text even if there is no thought of publication. Karl Marx thus often translated from English into German 'in such a way as to bring out what for him were the vital points of the writer's thought' (Nicolaus 1973: 66; see Large 2014: 184), and Pierre Hadot, who argued for philosophy as a 'way of life' (1995), developed a philosophical method that began with close reading of his classical sources followed by 'an equally exacting translation of these texts into French' (Chase 1995: vi), building his exegesis, interpretation and criticism upon translational practice; his English translator Michael Chase, therefore, translates all quotations in Hadot's texts from Hadot's own renderings, rather than seeking out published English versions, as he would otherwise do (Chase 1995: vi).

Weil read as a translator throughout her life. Not only did she turn to the New Testament in Greek, as indicated earlier, but she also translated it for her own use, exemplifying Chantal Wright's description of literary translation as a 'spiritual endeavour' (2016: 7). Her own translations are frequently found in her notebooks, essays and letters, and in a discussion of school subjects she stresses how translation can exemplify the need for attention that lies at the heart of her philosophy (see Cameron 2007: 119; Caprioglio Panizza 2022). If attention for Weil consists of the suspension of thought so that it can be penetrated by the object, as we discussed in Chapter 1 (WG 111), then 'wrong translations' can be explained by insufficient attention to the matter in hand:

> All wrong translations, all absurdities in geometry problems, all clumsiness of style, and all faulty connection of ideas in compositions and essays, all such things are due to the fact that thought has seized upon some idea too hastily. (WG 111)

The philosopher known for advocating the wait for God controversially notes that we 'just have to wait for the solution of a geometrical problem or the meaning of a Latin or Greek sentence to come into our mind' (WG 128); all the translator needs do is 'merely reject all inadequate words' (WG 113). It is reasonable to assume that she is speaking from experience. Study – including translation – can therefore be justified because it is a training in attention as defined earlier, a process that will guarantee success because of how the problem is approached.

To follow Weil is not to deny that linguistic competence is necessary for translation to take place, but it *is* to state that linguistic competence is not sufficient, that attention is also necessary. By 'attention', it should be inferred that Weil is speaking of more than the need to take care when writing a translation. Davis, for example, records writing 'walnuts' instead of 'hazelnuts' when translating a sentence in Gustave Flaubert's novel *Madame Bovary* because of 'momentary inattention' (2021: 271). Somebody might refer to this translation shift as an error of attention, but it is really an error in concentration. Davis was perfectly aware that Flaubert was writing about hazelnuts, yet wrote down the wrong word, something that can happen to the best of translators. Weil is seeking to define a more general relationship between translator and text, namely an attitude that parallels Willis Barnstone's description of literary translation:

A translation is a friendship between poets. There is a mystical union based on love and art. (1993: 166)

Such an attitude is passive, something that is represented in the French *attente*, which signifies both 'attending' and 'waiting'.[2] Certainly translation can feel passive when it is going well, and many translators report occasions when they feel minimally involved, as when Davis found that 'the diction more or less chose itself' when she was working on Marcel Proust's novel *Du côté de chez Swann* [Swann's Way] (2021: 223). Douglas Robinson uses Mihaly Csikszentmihalyi's notion of 'flow' to theorize such inspirational times when 'translating is fastest, most reliable, and most enjoyable' (2003: 213). A certain brain state is attained. We

---

[2]See the varying translations of the title of Weil's *Attente de Dieu* mentioned earlier.

can push Weil's idea even further. She advocates something like the demand of Eliot Weinberger:

> In its way a spiritual exercise, translation is dependent on the dissolution of the translator's ego: an absolute humility toward the text. (1987: 17)

Again there is the notion of translation as a spiritual endeavour (Wright 2016: 7), with attention at the heart of a practice that results in the dissolving of the ego, a process that sounds very like the 'decreation' that is another hallmark of Weil's later philosophy (cf. GG 26). As Anne Carson writes, Weil's process of decreation is a 'dislodging of herself from a centre where she cannot stay because staying there blocks God' (2006: 167). It is not necessary to share Weil's religious philosophy to find decreation a useful image for the translator. Translation may well be a suitable training for the mystic – one thinks of the centrality of translation in Christian traditions and of the role of a translator-saint such as Jerome – but its value in secular terms is beyond dispute. Weil's words show that translation is never a matter of mechanical transference, of only the competent use of a dictionary, but is rather something that demands a total engagement with the spirit of the text, and the willingness to reimagine it in another language (cf. Weinberger 1987: 34). Attention is not something supernatural in this context, but rather a perception of what it means to engage with an author.

It is also a concept that can function as a description of such an engagement.

Translation was an activity that Weil not only wrote about but also practised. Her essay on the *Iliad* as a poem of force includes a large amount of direct quotation from Homer (see IP). In twenty-four pages, she cites 265 lines (including parts of lines) in her own translation into French from Homeric Greek. Simone Pétrement recalls that Weil might spend half an hour translating a single line and asserts 'that never before has a translation so completely captured the human tenderness and pity that pervades the *Iliad*' (1976: 362). Pétrement's point is that Weil's rendering addresses and represents the spirit of the text. Weil does make translation errors, as noted by Christopher Benfey, who also argues that she fails to convey important aspects of Homer (2005). However, she remains loyal in her translations to the interpretation of the *Iliad* that is put forward in the essay.

Duncan Large argues that the category of philosopher-translator 'does not really exist in the same way that terms such as "poet-translator" and "author-translator" have gained currency in recent times' (2014: 183). He adds that there are, however, many examples of philosophers who have translated both philosophical and non-philosophical materials, citing (among others) Friedrich Schleiermacher's Plato and Walter Benjamin's Proust respectively (2014: 193). Weil fits Large's notion of the philosopher-translator and also goes beyond it, given that she was not only a philosopher-translator but also a *writer* of literature, as evidenced by this volume.

Finally, Weil is also translated. At the time of writing, not only are new texts by her still appearing in English, but existing English texts are also being retranslated now that Weil's work is in the public domain. We mentioned earlier that *Attente de Dieu* is available in three English versions, and a second translation of *The Need for Roots* is at the time of writing being prepared by Ros Schwartz (forthcoming). Readers will be able to compare Schwartz's Weil with the Weil of Arthur Wills (NR), whose translation of *L'enracinement* was first published in 1952, over seventy years ago. During this time, there has been a great deal of activity in Weil scholarship, and the English language itself has changed significantly, two factors that are important to consider when interpreting Weil today. All translations are interpretations – Meredith McKinney, for example, discussing her translation of Sei Shônagon's *The Pillow Book*, refers to 'my Sei Shônagon' (2005: 59) – and as of 2023, Anglophone readers will have both Wills's Weil and Schwartz's Weil when they wish to read this account of human obligations. Schwartz's version will also include paratextual material on the text and on the reasons why a new translation was needed. Such availability of plural translations is one mark of philosophical canonicity. If somebody wants to study, say, Plato's *Republic* in English, then there are a number of versions on the market, to say nothing of the renderings that have been made in the past, on which modern translators build. A plural life in translation may be another way in which Weil is shown to be of importance. The more translations, the better.

The writer

For Deborah Nelson, the success of Weil's posthumous writings can be explained by the way that she wrote (2017: 17), a contention in line with recent research that shows how the literary mind reacts to style (cf. Boase-Beier 2019: 34 ff.). Nelson stresses the impersonality of Weil's prose style (2017: 31), as seen in the frequent use of the third-person-singular indefinite personal pronoun *on* [one/they/you/people]. She refers to Weil's own description of her approach to writing, as laid out in a letter to Gustave Thibon:

> The real way of writing is to write as we translate. When we translate a text in some foreign language, we do not seek to add anything to it; on the contrary, we are scrupulously careful not to add anything to it. That is how we have to try to translate a text which is not written down. (GG xi)

The act of original composition is reconfigured as translation (see above), as not adding to a thought but saying exactly what needs to be said, just as Wittgenstein states that whatever can be said, can be said clearly (TL-P Preface). Such an insistence on clarity is found in Weil's 1937 essay 'The Power of Words', written in the Europe of Hitler and Stalin, when language was being deformed into propaganda. Weil pushes the argument even further to show that how texts are written has important political consequences:

> To clarify thought, to discredit the intrinsically meaningless words, and to define the use of others by precise analysis – to do this, strange though it may appear, might be a way of saving lives. (PW 4)

The words show how seriously she took her vocation as a writer, how she saw the story she was telling as important for the world.

It is impossible to get away from story (Wilson 2021: 8). Human beings exist in time and one thing follows another. Therefore, as we recount events, so stories get told. Frederic Jameson accordingly views narrative as the 'central function or instance of the human mind' (1981: 13). Weil constantly relates her thinking to the great stories of world literature. 'The Power of Words', for example, first appeared in French as 'Ne recommençons pas la guerre de Troie' [Let's not restart the Trojan War]. It draws on Homeric imagery, and the political misuse of language is paralleled with the figure of Helen of Troy:

The Greeks and Trojans massacred one another for ten years on account of Helen. Not one of them except the dilettante warrior Paris cared two straws about her. . . . For our contemporaries the role of Helen is played by words with capital letters. (PW 2–3)

Story is at both once particular and universal. Homer told two stories about the consequences of the abduction of one woman, but the tale of Troy has a universal relevance because human nature does not change over time:

The truth is that the role which we attribute to mysterious economic oligarchies was attributed by Homer's contemporaries to the gods of the Greek mythology. But there is no need of gods or conspiracies to make men rush headlong into the most absurd disasters. Human nature suffices. (PW 3)

Weil looks through the myths of both the Greek and the modern world to discern the truth that human nature is a sufficient cause of the misery around us. The reader is brought face to face with their own nature. Words with capital letters are shown for what they are. The reader is free to move on.

A tale

We include in this volume a story by Weil, a self-styled *conte* [tale] that she wrote in the winter of 1920–1, 'The Fairies of the Fire'. She was aged only eleven. Such tales can play a powerful role in childhood. When Weil was convalescing from an operation for appendicitis in 1912, her mother told her the story 'Marie in Gold and Marie in Tar', in which the protagonist is asked if she wants to enter through the door of gold or the door of tar. Marie chooses the latter, which turns out to be the right answer, and she is deluged in gold as a reward, whereas her stepsister asks to enter through the door of gold and is accordingly deluged in tar. Pétrement comments: 'Simone later said that this fairy tale had had an influence on her entire life' (1976: 9).

When discussing 'The Fairies of the Fire', exaggerated claims of genius ought to be avoided, given that it is such an early work, but it competently portrays a coherent world in which a significant action takes place, and features vivid depiction. The Emperor (or 'Megistos') of the Fairies, Phaidros, seems to have been murdered but reappears and takes vengeance. Many classic features of story are present: the hero, the shadow, the inciting incident, the ordeal and the triumph of and return of the hero (cf. McKee 1999). It is a fairy tale in two senses, both because it belongs to the fantasy folk genre and because it is actually about Fairies: Fairies made of fire, who live and move in flame. They are elemental, wild and unpredictable creatures, who dance on crackling logs, their exotic nature heightened by the use of Greek names for them and their traditions.[3] We can conjecture that Weil had become lost in thought while watching a log burn down in the cold months of the year and had imagined figures in the flames, which she describes in detail (if a little didactically) to an audience ignorant of the background mythology. She creates a conflict between light and dark, life and death, that points forward to the conflict between gravity and grace that dominates her mature thinking. At the end of the tale, harmony is restored to the burning world of the Fairies:

> Phaidros threw himself into the arms of his beautiful fiancée of the golden robe (which means marriage to the Fairies) and together they danced a furious 'orchesis', going faster than the wind, throwing out sparks that hid them from view, and so they sparkled, veiled by a golden dust.

It is a vision of beauty: the majestic Phaidos has a 'beautiful fiancée' and their furious dance is literally dazzling. For the sake of such beauty, Jaffier will save Venice.

---

[3]See the notes for an explanation of the Greek terms, which must have been taught to Weil by her brother André. The Greek language would become very important to Weil, who valorized Classical Greek civilization.

An essay

In her lifetime, Weil published relatively little, only 'around fifty essays in small leftist and factory journals' in her final eleven years (Nelson 2017: 15). The essay as a genre has its origins in the writings of Michel de Montaigne (1533–92), who wrote and collected short prose pieces that attempt to make the reader see life differently. In 'On experience', for example, he writes:

> We avoid wine from the bottom of the barrel; in Portugal they adore its savour; it is the drink of princes. In short each nation has several customs and practices which are not only unknown to another nation but barbarous and a cause of wonder. (2004: 384)

The elements of a classic essay – the French *essai* can signify an 'attempt' – are to be found in these two sentences: empirical observation followed by theoretical consideration. As a form, the essay continues to flourish in academic journals and in literary and political reviews and remains a way for writers to distil their thoughts: the novelist, short-story writer and translator Davis has recently published a second volume of essays, for example, in which the spirit of Montaigne is alive and well (2021).

The essay was also destined to become the standard means of assessing students in the humanities. Peter Womack has described it as 'the default genre for student writing', so that no matter what other ingenious forms of assessment arise, 'everyone returns, as if by a common homing instinct, to setting, marking and writing essays' (1993: 42). It is, therefore, no surprise that Alain, Weil's inspirational philosophy teacher at the Lycée Henri-IV, asked his students to submit an essay – the *topo* or short assignment – every three weeks on a subject of their choice, in the conviction that good writing meant good thinking (Yourgrau 2011: 32). We have included Weil's 1925 *topo*, 'The Tale of the Six Swans in Grimm', in this volume. Pétrement believes it to be the first piece of work by Weil that Alain thought to be excellent (1976: 58). Even though written when Weil was only sixteen, it has been viewed by critics as representative of her mature thought. Palle Yourgrau thus uses it as evidence that it is wrong to make a distinction, as some critics do, between an early political Weil and a later mystical Weil; for Yourgrau, the young Weil 'is no less rooted in the sky than are the six swans' (2011: 34), and even in 1925 'Simone is already Simone' (2011: 35).

As mentioned in Chapter 1, Alain showed Weil the importance of the close reading of primary texts and instilled in her a love of Plato that would never fade. Both influences are apparent in this essay, which is an exposition and analysis of a *conte* [tale] first recorded in writing in 1812 by Jacob and Wilhelm Grimm but coming from an older oral tradition. Weil's method follows Montaigne's practice of looking at a phenomenon and then reflecting on it. In the opening sentence, she also situates her work within a Platonic framework of interpretation:

> Among the most beautiful thoughts of Plato are those that he found by meditation upon myths.

In *The Republic*, for example, Socrates recounts the Myth of Er, which embodies a vision of the afterlife (616c ff.). (The Greek *muthos* can signify any sort of story and does not have some of the connotations of the word 'myth' in twenty-first-century English.) Weil proposes moving this approach to the present day:

> Who knows if there might not be ideas that could be drawn from our myths as well? Let's choose at random from the tales of Grimm, and let's take one of them for our subject, being careful to say along with Socrates: I shall say what is true in all that I shall say.

Socrates is seen as the paradigmatic philosopher on account of his restless interrogation of reality in all its forms and his desire to reach and tell the truth. Weil, in her role as a modern Socrates, chooses from Grimm the tale 'The Six Swans', in which an innocent young Queen saves her six brothers, who have been shape-shifted into swans. The Queen is able to lift the curse by sewing them shirts out of anemones and by remaining silent for six years, even in the face of accusations of infanticide made by the King's evil mother, who has in fact been kidnapping the children. The Queen's silence brings her perilously close to being burned at the stake. Nancy Huston notes how Weil was drawn to powerful young women who act to save their brothers, such as Antigone, Electra or the protagonist of this story (2005: 105), and it is possible to conjecture that Weil's own relationship with André played a role in her selection of text, given that she seems to have seen herself in the shadow of this mathematical genius. Her choice may not have been quite as random as she suggests.

The German folk tales and legends collected and shaped by the Grimm Brothers provide fertile material for Platonic interpretation. As Jack Zipes argues, they point beyond themselves, in line with Weil's view of myth:

> they provide hope that there is more to life than mastering the art of survival. Their 'once upon a time' keeps alive our utopian longing for a better world that can be created out of our dreams and actions. (2007: xlvi)

Weil similarly reads the story as one of hope. The virtue of the young Queen wins through and harmony is restored when the brothers regain their human form at the end and the family is reconstituted. Weil even omits one disturbing aspect of the tale. In the original, the wicked mother-in-law was 'tied to the stake and burned to ashes' (Grimm and Grimm 2007: 225.) Perhaps Weil's own longing for a better world led to this omission.

(She would see through the false utopias promised by Nazism and communism.)

Weil's philosophical interpretation of the story, which follows a lengthy exposition, is both highly original and challenging:

> The negation of action therefore possesses a virtue. This idea brings in the most profound thinking of the East. To act is never difficult: we always act too much and we constantly spread ourselves out in disordered acts. To make six shirts out of anemones, and to remain silent: this is our only means of gaining power.

Weil here looks outside the Western tradition – though her reference to 'the East' is vague and is not developed – in a way that is typical of a thinker who would come to equate Christ and Krishna. There also seems to be some sort of quietism at play, however, given that the triumph of virtue is seen as the result of the negation of acting. Quietism does not fit with the woman who would serve in the Spanish Civil War and who wanted to be parachuted into Nazi-occupied France. What is going on?

This *topo* can now be read in the light of Weil's later writings, which allows us to argue that the Queen is not doing nothing. She is attending. She is suffering. And by attending and suffering, she is saving. As Weil argues, if you give full attention to the second hand of a watch, you are not wasting your time. You are training yourself in attention, just as if you were patiently and humbly to read a text with a view to translating it. Her poem 'The Gate' similarly depicts waiting at the gate, rather than going through it, but at no point is it suggested that time is being wasted. As Wittgenstein asserts, sometimes we need to look rather than think (PI 66). The Queen does save her brothers by keeping silent and sewing, but at the end she *does* act by throwing the (almost) finished shirts at the swans, thereby restoring their original human shape (apart from that of the youngest, who retains one of his wings) and saving herself from the fire. Her deed parallels Paul's contention that he no longer lives, but Christ lives in him (Gal. 2.20). While Weil's interest in Christianity lay in the future, the figure of the Queen is reminiscent of the suffering Jesus, who remains silent before his accusers and tormenters (cf. Mk 14.61), and Weil herself made this connection shortly before she died:

> Silence of the girl in Grimm who saves the seven [*sic*] swans, her brothers. Silence of the Just Man in Isaiah . . . Silence of the Christ. (in O 802, our translation)

The 'girl in Grimm' is also compared to the Suffering Servant of Isaiah 53, who is cruelly mistreated and humiliated, but whose silent acceptance of affliction saves his people. (Isaiah was one of the few books of the Hebrew scriptures that Weil was able to accept.)

For Weil, myth ultimately shows a way to transcendent truth. It consists of 'one thing: placing into the body a truth that comes from the soul'. The essay concludes with a return to Plato, in the form of the myth of the naked and dead judges of the *Gorgias* (523e–527a), who pass judgement on naked and dead souls. Significantly, the six brothers in Grimm have been clothed by their sister as an integral part of their salvation: they are restored to *this* world, of the body. But final judgement will involve a total stripping in another world, of the soul, when the judged stand naked, according to Socrates, so that the scars of their sins will be visible. Similarly, the judges must be naked in order that no sin might be hidden, and their righteousness visible to all. Weil returned to this image at the end of her life:

> To be just it is necessary to be naked and dead – without imagination. That is why the model of justice has to be naked and dead. The cross alone is not open to imaginary imitation. (GG 88)

Weil distrusted the imagination. True justice involves divesting oneself of all that is imaginary and being attentive to judgement in total decreation, just like Christ, the world's judge, who hangs naked in a brutal public execution.

THE POEMS OF
SIMONE WEIL

À une jeune fille riche

Clymène, avec le temps je veux voir dans tes charmes
Sourdre de jour en jour, poindre le don des larmes.
Ta beauté n'est encore qu'une armure d'orgueil;
Les jours après les jours en feront de la cendre;
On ne te verra pas, éclatante, descendre,
Fière et masque baissé dans la nuit du cercueil.

À quel destin promise, en ta fleur passagère,
Glisses-tu? Quel destin? Quelle froide misère
Viendra serrer ton cœur à le faire crier?
Rien ne se lèvera pour sauver tant de grâce;
Les cieux restent muets pendant qu'un jour efface
Des traits purs, un teint doux qu'un jour a vus briller.

Un jour peut te blêmir la face, un jour peut tordre
Tes flancs sous une faim poignante; un frisson mordre
Ta chair frêle, naguère au creux de la tiédeur;
Un jour, et tu serais un spectre dans la ronde
Lasse qui sans arrêt par la prison du monde
Court, court, avec la faim au ventre pour moteur.

Comme un bétail la nuit par les bancs pourchassée,
Où trouver désormais ta main fine et racée,
Ton port, ton front, ta bouche avec son pli hautain?

To a Rich Girl

Clymene, with time's passing I shall see how your charms

fade away day by day, admit the gift of tears.

Your beauty is only the armour of your pride;

the days will follow days and turn it into ash,

and no one will see you, splendid, with lowered mask,

as you go down in pride into the coffin's dark night.

In this your brief flower, to which vowed destiny

do you glide? Unto which? And which cold misery

will come and grip your heart till it makes your heart scream?

But nothing shall arise to save all of this grace;

the Heavens are silent, and one day effaces

the pure traits, the sweet face that the day once saw gleam.

One day can make your face turn pale. One day can wring

your gut with a harrowing hunger; shudders sting

your so delicate flesh, once held within such warmth.

One day, and you will be a spectre wandering round,

weary and incessant in the prison of world,

driven on by hunger, just moving on and on.

Like night's wild animal, hunted down by the banks,

where will the future find your sweet and lovely hands,

your bearing, your forehead, the proud folds of your mouth?

L'eau brille. Trembles-tu? Pourquoi ce regard vide?
Trop morte pour mourir, reste donc, chair livide
Tas de loques prostré dans le gris du matin!

L'usine ouvre. Iras-tu peiner devant la chaîne?
Renonce au geste lent de ta grâce de reine.
Vite. Plus vite. Allons! Vite, plus vite. Au soir
Va-t'en, regards éteints, genoux brisés, soumise,
Sans un mot; sur ta lèvre humble et pâle qu'on lise
L'ordre dur obéi dans l'effort sans espoir.

T'en iras-tu, les soirs, aux rumeurs de la ville,
Pour quelques sous laisser souiller ta chair servile,
Ta chair morte, changée en pierre par la faim?
Elle ne frémit pas lorsqu'une main la frôle;
Les reculs, les sursauts sont rayés de ton rôle,
Les larmes sont un luxe où l'on aspire en vain.

Mais tu souris. Pour toi les malheurs sont des fables.
Tranquille et loin du sort de tes sœurs misérables,
Tu ne leur fis jamais la faveur d'un regard.
Tu peux, les yeux fermés, prodiguer les aumônes;
Ton sommeil même est pur de ces mornes fantômes
Et tes jours coulent clairs sous l'abris d'un rempart.

Des morceaux de papier, plus durs que les murailles,

Water gleams. You tremble? Why is your gaze empty?
Stay here, then, livid flesh, too dead even to die,
pile of rags lying sprawled in the grey of the dawn!

Will you work at the belt when the factory's open?
Renounce each slow gesture that graces you as queen.
Fast. Faster. Let us go! Fast. Faster. At evening,
defeated, you may leave: with dead eyes and bent knees
and no word. Let them read on humble and pale lips
the harsh order obeyed, effort without hoping.

So will you go, at dark, within the city's noise,
soiling your servile flesh for a couple of *sous*,
your dead flesh, that hunger has turned into a stone?
This flesh does not shudder at the touch of a hand.
Your role won't allow you to go on or go back.
Tears are a luxury, for which you hope in vain.

But you're smiling. For you, misfortunes are a myth.
You're tranquil and removed from wretched sisters' fate.
You do not even grant the favour of a look.
You may, with your closed eyes, be generous with alms;
even your sleep is free of all these sad phantoms,
and your days pass brightly under the rampart's shade.

These pieces of paper, harder than castle walls,

Te gardent. Qu'on les brûle, et ton cœur, tes entrailles,

Seront frappés de coups forts dont tout l'être est brisé.

Mais ce papier t'étouffe, il cache ciel et terre,

Il cache les mortels de Dieu. Sors de ta serre,

Nue et tremblante aux vents d'un univers glacé.

keep you safe. Let them burn: let your heart and entrails

be assaulted by blows that shatter your whole being. . .

But paper stifles you. It hides heaven and earth,

hides mortals and hides God. Come out of your greenhouse,

to the frozen world's wind; leave, naked and trembling.

Vers lus au Goûter de la Saint Charlemagne

Lycée Henry-IV (30 janvier 1926)

J'entends des chants, des cris, des appels et des rires;

Quels sont ces jeunes gens qui semblent si joyeux?

Quand pour nous les destins toujours deviennent pires,

Quelle est cette lueur que je vois dans leurs yeux?

Les uns sont des enfants, d'autres presque des hommes,

Mais un même bonheur illumine leur front;

Quels paradis voient-ils, éteints dès qu'on les nomme?

À quoi songent-ils donc, dans le trouble où nous sommes?

     Est-ce à ce qu'ils accompliront?

     Douce jeunesse, illuminée

     Des plus clairs regards du matin,

     Tu marches d'année en année

     A la rencontre du destin.

     Les yeux sur les pures étoiles,

     Tu vas vers l'avenir sans voiles;

     Tu marches parmi les clartés,

     Le regard libre et les mains vides,

     Au-devant des aubes splendides

     Qui se lèvent sur les cités.

     Ivre de l'ivresse du sage,

     Tu bois l'air pur, candide et clair;

Verses Read at the Feast of Saint Charlemagne

Lycée Henri-IV (30 January 1926)

I hear these songs, these shouts, and these calls and these laughs.

Who are these young people? And why is there such joy?

When destiny, for us, only gets worse and worse,

what then is the gleam that I see in each eye?

Some are only children, others are almost men,

but each forehead is lit by the same happiness.

What heaven remains theirs, though it dies at the name?

Of what are they dreaming within our present pain?

    Could it be of future success?

    Sweet youth, illuminated

    by the morning's clearest ray,

    you walk where years have been passed

    to meet with your destiny.

    With your eyes on the pure stars,

    You go forward without veils.

    You walk in the clarity,

    with open eyes, empty hands,

    to meet the coming splendid dawns

    rising over the cities.

    Intoxicated, a sage,

    you drink air: pure, clear, candid.

Tu crois ouïr un divin message

Dans ce silence plein d'éclairs;

Libre de parfums et de rêves,

Tu dédaignes les fleurs trop brèves,

Tu vas dans la paix de l'éveil,

Foulant la neige inviolée

Et ne voyant dans la vallée

Que les libres jeux du soleil.

Tu vas, forte, innocente et pure,

Tenant un glaive dans ta main;

Tu crois que l'éclat d'une armure

Siérait, sous ce soleil divin;

Libre et soudain comme un miracle,

Ton pur regard est un oracle

Pour tes aînés trop soucieux,

Qui se demandent, sans réponse,

Quels destins les astres annoncent

À ces jeunes silencieux.

Car les destins présents sont mornes et tragiques;

Le pain au citoyen parfois vient à manquer;

Le peuple, fatigué des luttes politiques,

Déjà s'irrite et tremble et commence à gronder.

Au loin notre pays voit, en de mornes guerres,

Combattre ses soldats encore presque enfants;

You seem to hear God's message
in silence full of lightning.
Free of perfumes and of dreams,
you treat the brief flowers with scorn.
You walk in the peace of the day,
treading inviolate snow
and all that you see below
are games of the sun at play.

Strong, you go: innocent, pure,
holding a glaive in your hand;
you believe that bright armour
will dazzle, under God's sun;
free and sudden miracle,
your gaze is an oracle
for these, your anxious elders,
who wonder, without reply
what fate the stars prophesy
to the young, silent walkers.

For present destiny is sombre and tragic;
bread for the citizen will sometimes disappear;
the people are worn down by fights in politics;
angrily they tremble, then they begin to roar.
Our country sees afar, in the most sombre wars,
her soldiers in combat, themselves almost children.

Ici, de durs soucis font les regards austères;

Que peuvent donc songer, dans toutes ces misères,

　　　Ces jeunes hommes triomphants?

Peut-être devant eux ils voient, comme en un rêve,

Passer cet Empereur dont nous fêtons le nom;

Ils voient des bras levés qui s'abattent sans trêve,

Entendent des coups sourds plus beaux que les canons.

L'on brandissait alors Durandal et Joyeuse;

Les glaives au soleil scintillaient par éclairs;

Et sans cesse passaient, troupe victorieuse,

Bien droits sur leurs chevaux, dans leur joie orgueilleuse,

　　　Les chevaliers au regard clair.

Ils luttent, ces héros, hardiment, d'homme à homme,

Le glaive teint de sang, mais le cœur toujours pur;

Au ciel l'ange sourit au soldat qui le nomme,

Et le guerrier combat, plus ardent et plus sûr.

C'est pour Dieu que l'on lutte, et pour la douce France;

Autour du chevalier qui meurt, joignant les mains,

Les trois vierges de Dieu viennent, beau chœur qui danse,

La Charité, la Foi, la candide Espérance,

　　　Pour lui dévoiler les destins.

Cependant que ses pairs l'emportent vers la terre,

Douce terre de France où son corps dormira! . . .

Here, the heaviest cares make for austerest frowns;
of what, then, in the midst of all these miseries,

    can these young victors be dreaming?

Perhaps, before them now, they see, as in a dream,
the Emperor passing, whose feast we celebrate:
they hear the heavy blows, much nobler than cannons;
they see the weapons raised, striking without respite.
Durandal and Joyeuse in those days were brandished;
every glaive sparkled and shone bright in the sun;
and, with no end in sight, victorious troops passed
upright upon horseback, in the joy of their pride;

    all the knights with fair countenance.

They struggle, these heroes, boldly and man to man,
the glaive is stained with blood but the heart is still pure;
see heaven's angel smile to soldiers who name him,
while the warrior fights on, more ardent and more sure.
The struggle is for God, and for our gentle France;
and hands are united around the knight who dies
by God's own three virgins, a fair chorus in dance:
Charity, Faith and Hope, Hope that is genuine,

    and they reveal his destiny.

And yet his peers will lay the soldier in the earth
the gentle earth of France where his body will rest!. . .

Puis retournent combattre; et de nouveau la guerre
Gronde, et l'on rivalise à qui le vengera.
Le mort s'ajoute au mort; d'autres blessés sans cesse,
Par le glaive frappés, s'ajoutent aux blessés;
Puis, sans même sentir ce glaive qui les blesse,
Se lèvent pour frapper, frapper, avec ivresse,
  Tant, que leurs bras en sont lassés.

Et le jeune homme ardent qui songe à Charlemagne
Veut, à son tour, combattre, et lutter, et mourir;
Marcher, marcher sans fin, par val et par montagne,
A la suite d'un chef, et sans songer à fuir.
Un sang jeune et bouillant dans ses veines ardentes
S'épand; il ne sait pas que les temps sont passés
Où l'homme frappait l'homme avec ses mains sanglantes
Et nourrissait sans fin ses ivresses brûlantes
  Avec des crânes fracassés!

Le jeune homme, à présent, ne peut plus, dans la guerre,
Assouvir son besoin d'agir et de lutter;
Les soldats d'aujourd'hui luttent – combat sévère! –
Sans glaive, dans la boue, et sans pouvoir frapper.
Mais s'il ne peut rêver de suivre cette route,
Mais s'il ne peut rêver d'imiter ces soldats,
Qu'il ne s'afflige pas! et plutôt qu'il écoute
En lui sourdre une voix plus forte que le doute,
  Qui l'appelle à d'autres combats.

They return to the fight; and once again the war
roars, and they all compete as to who will avenge.
Dead are joined to the dead. Others receive fresh wounds
and the cut of the glaive adds them to the wounded;
then, quite insensible to where the glaive has struck,
they rise to strike again, to strike in drunkenness,

    until their arms become wearied.

And the ardent young man who dreams of Charlemagne
desires, in his own turn, to join the fight and die;
to march and march and march, by valley and mountain,
following a leader, without a thought of flight.
Within his ardent veins, a young and boiling blood
swells up; he does not know that the time has now gone
when, with bloody hands a man could strike a man,
and endlessly nourish the frenzy that then burned

    on human skulls, smashed and broken!

No longer can the youth go off to find a war
to satisfy his need to do great deeds and fight;
the soldiers of today face a fight more severe,
without glaives, in the mud, and unable to strike.
But if he cannot dream of following that route,
and if he cannot dream of following soldiers,
let him not be distressed! But let him rather heed
to his own inner voice that is stronger than doubt

    and that calls him to different wars.

Car ces temps ne sont plus où l'homme allait en rêve

S'enivrant vainement de vaines actions;

Nous, il nous faut combattre en des combats sans trêve,

Plus beaux que les combats entre les nations.

Ce qu'il nous faut dompter, nous autres, c'est le monde;

Étreignant l'univers de notre forte main,

Il nous faut établir le droit, la paix féconde,

Et partout imposer notre empreinte profonde

     Sur les choses et le destin!

Partez donc, jeunes gens, dans l'ardeur de votre âge,

Partez, fors et virils, pour des combats si beaux;

Par deux grandes vertus, Patience et Courage,

Soyez vainqueurs de tout, et même des tombeaux.

Plutôt que Charlemagne, invoquez cette sainte

Qui fut par son grand cœur plus forte que la mort;

Telle que l'invoquait le Français dans sa crainte,

Lorsqu'il la regardait, sans menace et sans plainte,

     Veiller sur la Ville qui dort!

For the days of such dreams are now in the past,
when vainly men got drunk on actions that were vain.
As for us, we must fight in the war that will last,
nobler than the combats nation against nation.
The task that awaits us is to tame the whole world,
to seize with our strong hands the entire universe.
Law and a lasting peace are to be established
and our profound footstep must be imposed,

    on all things and all destinies!

Go forth, then, young people, in your youthful ardour,
leave, so strong and virile, for the noble combat.
May the two great virtues of Patience and Courage,
make you conquerors of all, and even of the tomb.
Rather than Charlemagne, evoke this other saint
who was by her great heart even stronger than death,
the one whom the Frenchman invoked in his dire need,
as he regarded her, without threat or complaint

    watch over the City that sleeps!

Éclair

Que le ciel pur sur ma face m'envoie,
Ce ciel de longs nuages balayé,
Un vent si fort, vent à l'odeur de joie,
Que naisse tout, de rêves nettoyé:

Naîtront pour moi les humaines cités
Qu'un soufflé pur a fait nettes de brume,
Les toits, les pas, les cris, les cent clartés,
Les bruits humains, ce que le temps consume.

Naîtront les mers, la barque balancée,
Le coup de rame et les feux de la nuit;
Naîtront les champs, la javelle lancée;
Naîtront les soirs, l'astre qui l'astre suit.

Naîtront la lampe et les genoux ployés,
L'ombre, le heurt aux détours de la mine;
Naîtront les mains, les durs métaux broyés;
Le fer mordu dans un cri de machine.

Le monde est né; vent, soufflé afin qu'il dure!
Mais il périt recouvert de fumées.
Il m'était né dans une déchirure
De ciel vert pâle au milieu des nuées.

Lightning

Let the pure sky on my face send to me
– this sky where long clouds have now been swept clear –
a wind that is strong and perfumed by joy,
so that all can be born, cleansed of each dream:

let human cities be born for me now,
which a pure breathing has made free of brume:
the rooftops, footsteps, cries, the hundred glows,
all the human noises consumed by time.

Let seas and the rolling vessel be born,
and the beat of oars and the night's own fire;
let the fields be born and the swathes be thrown;
let evenings be born, star to follow star.

Let the lamp be born and the knee on the ground,
and shadows in every twist of the mine;
let hands be born, let harsh metals be crushed,
iron be bitten by the machine's scream.

The world is born: blow, wind, keep it alive!
It perishes, covered again by fumes.
It was born to me within the divide
of a pale green sky, a parting of clouds.

Prométhée

Un animal hagard de solitude,

Sans cesse au ventre un rongeur qui le mord,

Le fait courir, tremblant de lassitude,

Pour fuir la faim qu'il ne fuit qu'à la mort;

Cherchant sa vie au travers de bois sombres;

Aveugle quand la nuit répand ses ombres;

Au creux des rocs frappé de froids mortels;

Ne s'accouplant qu'au hasard des étreintes;

En proie aux dieux, criant sous leurs atteintes –

Sans Prométhée, hommes, vous seriez tels.

Feu créateur, destructeur, flamme artiste!

Feu, héritier des lueurs du couchant!

L'aurore monte au cœur du soir trop triste;

Le doux foyer a joint les mains; le champ

A pris le lieu des broussailles brûlées.

Le métal dur jaillit dans les coulées,

Le fer ardent plie et cède au marteau.

Une clarté sous un toit comble l'âme.

Le pain mûrit comme un fruit dans la flamme.

Qu'il vous aima, pour faire un don si beau!

Il donna roue et levier. O merveille!

Le destin plie au poids faible des mains.

Prometheus

An animal, haggard with solitude,

with a rodent in its stomach, biting,

making it run, trembling with lassitude

to flee the hunger it flees by dying;

looking for life in the sombre wood;

blinded when the night spreads out its shade;

struck by mortal cold below the rocks;

and coupling only when chance allows;

prey to the gods, screaming under their blows –

men, so you would be without Prometheus.

Creative fire, destroyer and artist!

Fire, heir of the setting sun's rays!

The dawn rises to the sad evening's heart;

the gentle hearth joins its hands; the fields

have taken the place of burned undergrowth.

Harsh metal flows now within the casts,

and iron yields to the hammer's craft.

The soul is filled by light under the roof.

Within the flame, bread ripens like fruit.

How he loved you, to make you such a gift!

O miracle! He gave you wheel and lever!

Destiny bends to the feeble weight of hands.

Le besoin craint de loin la main qui veille

Sur les leviers, maîtresse des chemins.

O vents des mers vaincus par une toile!

O terre ouverte au soc, saignant sans voile!

Abîme où frêle une lampe descend!

Le fer court, mord, arrache, étire et broie,

Docile et dur. Les bras portent leur proie,

L'univers lourd qui donne et boit le sang.

Il fut l'auteur des rites et du temple,

Cercle magique à retenir les dieux

Loin de ce monde; ainsi l'homme contemple,

Seul et muet, le sort, la mort, les cieux.

Il fut l'auteur des signes, des langages.

Les mots ailés vont à travers les âges

Par monts, par vaux, mouvoir les cœurs, les bras.

L'âme se parle et tâche à se comprendre.

Ciel, terre et mer se taisent pour entendre

Deux amis, deux amants parler tout bas.

Plus lumineux fut le présent des nombres.

Les spectres, les démons s'en vont mourant.

La voix qui compte a su chasser les ombres.

L'ouragan même est calme et transparent.

Au ciel sans fond prend place chaque étoile;

Sans un mensonge elle parle à la voile.

Need fears afar the hand that looks over
the levers, and is mistress of the routes.
O winds of seas, vanquished by a sail!
O soil, open naked to the ploughshare!
Abyss, where the frail lamp may descend!
Iron runs, bites, tears, pulls and crushes,
docile and hard. The heavy universe
is taken as prey. It gives and drinks blood.

He was the author of rites and the temple,
the magic circle that would keep the gods
far from this world; and so man contemplates
fate, death and the sky, alone and mute.
He was the author of signs and languages.
Winged words travel across the ages,
over peaks and valleys, to move hearts and arms.
The soul speaks to itself, tries to understand.
Heaven, earth and sea silently hear the sound
of two friends or lovers, talking in low tones.

More luminous was the presence of numbers.
Spectres and demons fade away, dying.
The counting voice has chased away shadows.
There is calm, even in the hurricane.
Every star takes its place in the bottomless sky
and talks to the sail without a lie.

L'acte s'ajoute à l'acte; rien n'est seul

Tout se répond sur la juste balance.

Il naît des chants purs comme le silence.

Parfois du temps s'entrouvre le linceul.

L'aube est par lui une joie immortelle.

Mais un sort sans douceur le tient plié.

Le fer le cloue au roc; son front chancelle;

En lui, pendant qu'il pend crucifié,

La douleur froide entre comme une lame.

Heures, saisons, siècles lui rongent l'âme,

Jour après jour fait défaillir son cœur.

Son corps se tord en vain sous la contrainte;

L'instant qui fuit disperse aux vents sa plainte;

Seul et sans nom, chair livrée au malheur.

Act is added to act; nothing is alone.

All is balanced on scales of justice.

Songs are born, as pure as the silence.

Sometimes the shroud of time will fall open.

Dawn – because of him – is immortal bliss.

But a pitiless fate holds him in its hand.

Iron nails him to the rock; his brow trembles.

Through him, as he hangs there crucified,

cuts a cold pain, like the blade of a sword.

Hours, seasons, centuries gnaw at his soul

and his heart grows weaker with each passing day.

His body twists in vain, under constraint;

and his screams are heard only by the wind;

alone, nameless, flesh bound by affliction.

À un jour

Hors des brumes le jour se lève
Par-delà les cimes des monts.

L'univers va chasser le rêve;
Qu'il paraisse! Adieu les démons!

Quand la clarté pâle et glacée
Pénètre l'âme, traversée
Soudain de ses traits déchirants,
Du frisson de chaque herbe frêle
Qu'un silence monte et se mêle
Sans terme aux déserts transparents!

Quel cœur ne fend, si la subite
Et douce atteinte du matin
Défait l'ombre où tout bas s'agite
Doute, remords, peur du destin?
La grâce lui fait mal; il saigne
Devant les plaines où l'eau baigne
Des plis de brouillard délicat,
La ramure qui tremble nue,
L'aile qui glisse suspendue,
L'air inondé d'un faible éclat.

Jour naissant, jour fait de rosée,
Si clair dans l'âme et dans les cieux,
Toute cette splendeur posée

To a Day

Out of mists arises the day,

beyond the peaks of the mountains.

The universe hunts dreams away.

Let day appear! Farewell, demons!

When pale and frozen clarity

penetrates every soul, crossed by

the day's sudden and searing traits . . .

then let silence ascend and blend

endlessly with shining desert,

out of the shiver of frail grass!

Which heart would not break, if the quick

and gentle jolting of morning

dispels shadows of infinite

doubt, remorse, fear of destiny?

Grace hurts the heart; and it will bleed

before the plains, where water bathes

from folds of the delicate fog

the branches that tremble naked;

the wing that glides there, suspended;

the air flooded by the weak light.

Nascent day, day made out of dew,

so clear in the soul and the skies,

where the very splendour of you

Comme une caresse en tous lieux

Nous reviendra tendre et limpide.

Le soir à travers l'air fluide

En comblera le pré mouillé.

Mais avant que le soir descende

Et parmi nous calme s'étende,

O jour, que tu seras souillé!

*

Chaque minute, ô jour qui monte!

Quand elle a fui d'un vol muet

Après elle laisse la honte

Que recueille l'instant qui naît.

Partout quelque bouche soudaine

S'ouvre et vient ternir d'une haleine

Les jours et les douces saisons

D'êtres hier encor sans larmes

Qui maintenant n'ont plus qu'alarmes

Vains travaux, détresse et prisons.

Quel effort tord les destinées

Dont l'or, le fer, le sort, les lois

Écrasent les vastes années

Dans l'espace d'un peu de voix!

Quand les lèvres inattentives

in a universal caress
will return, tender and limpid.
Evening, in the air so fluid,
will possess the dew-soaked meadow.
But before evening comes to us,
and its calm reaches out through us,
o day, how tarnished you'll become!

                              *

Each minute, o arising day!
Each minute will flee in mute flight,
leaving behind itself the shame,
welcomed by the new-born moment.
Everywhere will appear a mouth,
coming to tarnish with its breath
the days and the gentlest seasons
of beings who've not shed a tear,
who'll only know anxiety,
vain works, and distress, and prisons.

What effort wrings those destinies
where gold, iron, fate and command
can crush the vast, unending years
in the space of a spoken word!
When lips fail to pay attention

Laissent sur les foules captives

Tomber ces mots, si lourds de temps,

Les heures croulent en poussières;

La clarté touche les paupières,

Elle a déserté les instants.

Pourquoi blesser de ton aurore

Les yeux des vaincus, jour mort-né?

Ils sont las qu'il leur faille encore

Voir luire un soleil condamné.

Un jour mort est trop long à vivre.

L'aube amère ordonne d'en suivre

Le cours affreux sans chanceler.

Le cœur, les genoux leur défaillent.

Il faut pourtant debout qu'ils aillent

Où l'âme ne veut pas aller.

Mille fois mille âmes désertes

Saluent ce jour déjà perdu.

Ces mille et mille jours inertes

Sont un jouet vil et vendu.

Quelques joueurs, hantés d'images,

Le regard au lointain des âges,

Ignorent que le jour paraît.

L'aube et le soir ne sont que songe

Si comme un glaive au cœur n'en plonge

La brève et lumineuse paix.

and offer the captive nation
words that are loaded down with time,
then the hours will crawl in the dust;
brightness will touch every eyelid,
but the moment will not return.

Why do you injure with your dawn
these conquered eyes, o still-born day?
To have to watch a condemned sun
shine yet again makes them weary.
One dead day is too long to live.
The bitter dawn asks them to keep
their dreaded course and not falter.
Their hearts and knees are far too faint.
And yet they must stand and set out,
go where the soul will not wander.

A thousand souls, a thousand times,
salute a day already lost.
Thousands of days, deserted, numb,
are a toy that is vile and sold.
Players, haunted by images,
looking at some far-off ages,
do not know that the day's arrived.
Dawn and evening are but a dream
if a brief and luminous peace
does not pierce the heart like a glaive.

Aveugles, ils foulent et brassent

Avenirs, passés et présents,

Toujours, sans savoir, quoi qu'ils fassent,

Dans leur faim des jours et des ans,

Se rassasier d'aucun nombre.

Leur main croit, se crispant dans l'ombre,

Tenir les siècles malheureux.

En vain l'axe des cieux est juste.

Jour frêle et sacré, jour auguste,

Jour, tu n'es pas éclos pour eux.

Pour qui, hélas, viens-tu d'éclore?

Ces jeunes êtres effondrés,

Voulais-tu les baigner d'aurore

Parmi les champs non labourés?

Du gris sur leurs faces boueuses,

Loin des mains pour eux seuls soigneuses,

Ils sont à terre pour toujours,

La bouche ouverte sans prière,

L'œil insensible à la lumière,

Dépouillés de leur part de jours.

D'autre, nus, sont couverts des gouttes

De l'aube au travers des chemins.

Vers tous les habitants des routes

Ils tendirent leurs vaines mains.

Blind, they surge forward and they blend
the present, the past, the future,
but always remain ignorant
– in their days and years of hunger –
of how to eat, be satisfied.
In the darkness, they clench their fists,
think they hold the unhappy age.
Heaven's axis is just – in vain.
Frail and sacred day, noble day:
day, for them you bring no escape.

For whom, alas, have you come down?
For those who are young and battered?
Did you want to bathe them in dawn,
among fields that no one has ploughed?
Their muddy faces are so grey.
They are far from hands that might care.
Their unpraying mouths are agape.
They are always on this planet.
Their eyes do not react to light.
They've been robbed of their part in days.

Some are naked, covered in drops
of the dawn from across the path.
But in vain they stretch out their hands
to those who live along the road.

On charge comme de la terre
Les os qu'a rongés la misère,
Que nulle terre n'a nourris.
Et d'autres, que d'autres qui gisent. . .
Les jours passés leur interdisent
De te voir, jour qui leur souris.

Jour sans force, la pierre même
Tu ne pourras la traverser.
Un mur te retire à qui t'aime;
Et des murs en plomb vont peser
Jusqu'à la nuit sur les poitrines.
Du tumulte lourd des usines,
Des marchés de chair à souiller,
Du fond des prisons immuables,
Montent les regards misérables.
Quel rayon daigne les baigner?

Tout est clos sur la foule obscure
Dont tremblent les membres liés.
Aux destins soumis à l'injure,
Aux longs efforts humiliés,
Que les claires plaines sont grises!
Même dans la tiédeur des brises,
Même en marche au milieu d'un champ,
L'opprobre et la stupeur amère

The bones that were gnawed by distress
are heavy like the soil itself,
though no soil ever nourished them.
And so many others just lie. . .
They are forbidden by passed days
to see you, day that greeted them.

Day without power: for you cannot
even make your way through a stone.
A wall keeps you from your beloved;
and such walls of lead will weigh down
on every breast until nightfall.
From the factories' heavy tumult,
from the markets where flesh is soiled,
from deep, immutable prisons:
how many eyes are now gazing?
Will they ever be bathed by light?

It is over for those trembling
and linked within the darkened crowd.
And how grey are the purest plains,
where destiny is submitted
to injury, where act is shame!
Even when the breezes are warm,
even in a field, out walking,
the disgrace and bitter stupor

Auront interdit ciel et terre

Tout ce jour au jour caressant.

Mais plus de nuit couvre l'espèce

Qui fourmille par les cités

Des êtres à la chair épaisse

Dont l'esprit dort sous les clartés.

Ils ne tressaillent qu'à la foudre

Dès que pour détruire et dissoudre

Elle tombe les traverser.

Ce jour heureux qui vient de naître,

Nul n'aura-t-il su le connaître

Lorsque son cours devra cesser?

*

Faible rire brillant des larmes,

Début d'un jour parmi les jours,

Viens, prends-nous, lève les alarmes,

Monte, illumine, allume, accours!

Ta flamme glisse d'heure en heure;

Ton aile à l'éclat calme effleure

Tour à tour les pâles pays.

Les airs sont en fleurs sur tes traces.

Qu'une fois par les lents espaces

On veille alors que tu jaillis!

will have forbidden sky and earth
the caress of day in the day.

But still more night covers the race
that swarms through the cities like ants,
these beings with the thickness of flesh,
whose spirits sleep under the light.
They only shiver at thunder
when it falls as their destroyer,
to pierce them through as it hits.
The happy day, only just born,
will it ever have been known,
before having to find its end?

*

Feeble laugh, brilliant in tears,
start of a day amongst the days,
come and take us, lift the alarms,
rise, shine on us, kindle, make haste!
Your flame glides from hour into hour,
your wing, shining and calm, will touch
all the pale countries, each in turn.
The air that follows is in flower.
If only once, in this slow clime
we might be awake when you burst!

Que d'un chant d'ange l'aube appelle

Un cœur soudain muet et clair

A la douceur de la nouvelle

Qui palpite éparse dans l'air.

Que ce long jour lui soit le pacte

Qui joigne sans fin l'âme exacte

À la balance innée aux cieux.

O long jour qu'il va boire avide,

Passe et le comble par un vide

Qui fait de lui l'égal des dieux.

En vain vont pâlir sur la plaine

Ce soir les suprêmes lueurs.

Le ciel en vain mouvant entraîne

Les sereines heures ailleurs.

Ce jour de céleste silence

Livre à jamais au monde immense

Un esprit transpercé d'amour,

Même si son moment s'apprête

Et si le sort aveugle arrête

Que soit venu son dernier jour.

Let dawn's angelic song summon
the heart, which becomes mute and clear
at the sweetness of the message
that quivers in the scattered air.
Let the long day be the new pact
that joins forever the exact
soul unto heaven's inner scales.
O long day that the heart will drink,
pass! And fill the heart with a void
that will make it the gods' equal.

In vain will the ultimate glow
go pale this evening on the plain.
The sky will move and drag in vain
elsewhere, these serenest hours.
This day of heavenly silence
offers forever the cosmos
a spirit that love has pierced through,
even if its moment draws close,
even if blind fate has decreed
that this is the last of the days.

La mer

Mer docile au frein, mer soumise en silence,

Mer éparse, aux flots enchaînés pour toujours,

Masse offerte au ciel, miroir d'obéissance;

Pour y tisser chaque nuit des plis nouveaux,

Les astres au loin sans effort ont puissance.

Lorsque le matin vient combler tout l'espace,

Elle accueille et rend le don de la clarté.

Un éclat léger se pose à la surface.

Elle s'étend dans l'attente et sans désir,

Sous le jour qui croît, resplendit et s'efface.

Les reflets du soir feront luire soudaine

L'aile suspendue entre le ciel et l'eau.

Les flots oscillants et fixés à la plaine,

Où chaque goutte à son tour monte et descend,

Demeurent en bas par la loi souveraine.

La balance aux bras secrets d'eau transparente

Se pèse elle-même, et l'écume, et le fer,

Juste sans témoin pour chaque barque errante.

Sur le navire un fil bleu trace un rapport,

Sans aucune erreur dans sa ligne apparente.

Mer vaste, aux mortels malheureux sois propice,

Pressés sur tes bords, perdus sur ton désert.

A qui va sombrer parle avant qu'il périsse.

Entre jusqu'à l'âme, ô notre sœur la mer;

Daigne la laver dans tes eaux de justice.

The Sea

Sea, docile at ebb. Sea, slave to the silence.
Sparse sea, chained for eternity to the flows.
Mass open to sky, mirror of obedience.
The distant stars, effortlessly, have the power
to weave into you every night these new folds.

When morning arrives to fill up all the space,
it takes and gives back the gift of clarity.
A faint gleam comes down to rest on the surface.
It spreads out in attention, without desire,
under a day that grows; and gleams; and then fades.

Reflections of evening will illuminate
the wing suspended between sky and water.
Fixed to the plane are the waves that oscillate,
where each drop in turn will first rise, then descend,
remaining below, as sovereign laws dictate.

Transparent scales with secret arms of water,
weighing themselves, and the foam, and the iron.
Just (without witness) to barques that are erring.
On each ship is a blue line, a connection
with no error on the visible border.

Vast sea, show favour to mortals: afflicted,
crushed at your edge, and lost within your desert.
Speak to those who sink, before they are drowned.
Enter into our soul, o sea, our sister.
Deign to wash it clean, with waters that are just.

Nécessité

Le cercle des jours du ciel désert qui tourne

Parmi le silence aux regards des mortels,

Gueule ouverte ici-bas, où chaque heure enfourne

Tant de cris si suppliants et si cruels;

Tous les astres lents dans les pas de leur danse,

Seule danse fixe, éclat muet d'en haut,

Sans forme malgré nous, sans nom, sans cadence,

Trop parfaits, que ne revêt aucun défaut;

À eux suspendus, notre colère est vaine.

Calmez notre soif si vous brisez nos cœurs.

Clamant et désirant, leur cercle nous traîne;

Nos maîtres brillants furent toujours vainqueurs.

Déchirez les chairs, chaînes de clarté pure.

Cloués sans un cri sur le point fixe au Nord,

L'âme nue exposée à toute blessure,

Nous voulons vous obéir jusqu'à la mort.

Necessity

Circle of days in the desert-sky that turns
within silence to the gaze of the mortals,
to mouths that gape below, where each hour includes
so many cries, so imploring, so cruel;

all the slow stars in the slow pace of their dance,
the only fixed dance, the mute light from above,
formless despite us, without name or cadence,
too perfect for any fault to be alive:

to them, hanging there, our anger is in vain.
Satisfy our thirst, if you would break our hearts.
Claiming, desiring, their circle drags us on;
our shining masters were always victorious.

Tear up the flesh, you chains of pure clarity.
Nailed without a cry on the northern fixed point,
the naked soul exposed to all injury,
we desire to obey you, unto death.

Les astres

Astres en feu peuplant la nuit les cieux lointains,

Astres muets tournant sans voir toujours glacés,

Vous arrachez hors de nos cœurs les jours d'hier,

Vous nous jetez aux lendemains sans notre aveu,

Et nous pleurons et tous nos cris vers vous sont vains.

Puisqu'il le faut, nous vous suivrons, les bras liés,

Les yeux tournés vers votre éclat pur mais amer.

À votre aspect toute douleur importe peu.

Nous nous taisons, nous chancelons sur nos chemins.

Il est là dans le cœur soudain, leur feu divin.[1]

---

[1]Trois autres versions du vers final:

  Ils sont là dans le cœur soudain, les feux divins.
  Vous levez l'âme à vous sans peine, astres divins.
  Vous nous levez à vous sans peine, astres divins.

The Stars

Stars are on fire, peopling the night of distant skies,

unspeaking stars, turning blindly, always frozen:

you tear away our yesterdays out of our heart,

you propel us to tomorrow without our leave,

and so we weep, but cries to you are of no use.

Since we must, we follow you, with our arms in chains,

turning our eyes towards your pure but bitter light.

Under your aspect, how little all suffering means.

We are silent and we stagger upon our ways.

Then in the heart so suddenly, their divine fires.[2]

---

[1]Three other versions of the last line:
So suddenly within the heart, the divine fires.
You raise the soul safely to you, o divine stars.
You raise us up safely to you, o divine stars.

La porte

Ouvrez-nous donc la porte et nous verrons les vergers,
Nous boirons leur eau froide où la lune a mis sa trace.
La longue route brûle ennemie aux étrangers.
Nous errons sans savoir et ne trouvons nulle place.

Nous voulons voir des fleurs. Ici la soif est sur nous.
Attendant et souffrant, nous voici devant la porte.
S'il le faut nous romprons cette porte avec nos coups.
Nous pressons et poussons, mais la barrière est trop forte.

Il faut languir, attendre et regarder vainement.
Nous regardons la porte; elle est close, inébranlable.
Nous y fixons nos yeux; nous pleurons sous le tourment;
Nous la voyons toujours; le poids du temps nous accable.

La porte est devant nous; que nous sert-il de vouloir?
Il vaut mieux s'en aller abandonnant l'espérance.
Nous n'entrerons jamais. Nous sommes las de la voir.
La porte en s'ouvrant laissa passer tant de silence

Que ni les vergers ne sont parus ni nulle fleur;
Seul l'espace immense où sont le vide et la lumière
Fut soudain présent de part en part, combla le cœur,
Et lava les yeux presque aveugles sous la poussière.

The Gate

Open the gate for us, and we shall see the orchards.
We shall drink cold water where the moon has left its trace.
The long road is burning and hostile to the strangers.
We err without knowing and we never find our place.

We want to see the flowers. Here the thirst is upon us.
Waiting and suffering, here we are before the gate.
If we must, we shall break down this gate with all our blows.
We press and then we push; but this barrier is too great.

We must languish and wait and we must keep watch in vain.
We look upon the gate; it is closed and too heavy.
We fix our eyes on it; we weep under the torment.
We keep it in our view; we're crushed by time's gravity.

The gate is before us; what's the use of our desire?
It is better to leave and to give up on all hope.
We shall never get in. Watching it has made us tired.
So much silence came out when the gate was once opened

that neither the orchards nor the flowers have appeared;
only the immense space of the void and of the light,
which then became present and that overwhelmed the heart,
and bathed our eyes at last, almost blinded by the dust.

FOUR EXCERPTS FROM
VENICE SAVED

Jaffier (I)

Il me faut partir abandonné,

Éperdu d'opprobre et de détresse.

Mes amis meurent trahis par moi.

Ceux que j'ai sauvés par ma pitié,

Après m'avoir pris l'honneur, me chassent.

La clarté du jour me fait souffrir.

Je suis las d'être les yeux baissés.

Si je veux mourir, le cœur me manque.

Je ne voudrais pas devenir fou.

Jaffier (I)

Abandoned, I am forced to depart,

overcome with disgrace and distress.

My friends will die, all betrayed by me.

Those whom I have saved by my pity,

having robbed me of honour, ban me.

The brightness of day makes me suffer.

I am weary of my lowered eyes.

If I want to die, I lack the heart.

I do not wish to become insane.

Jaffier (II)

Je m'en vais sans amis, chassé, privé de mon honneur.

On ne veut plus de moi, maintenant qu'on m'a tout fait perdre.

Où puis-je me tourner? Qui voudra recevoir un traître,

Puisque ceux qu'a sauvés ma trahison vont me chasser?

Cela ne se peut pas. Je veux parler à votre maître.

Ceux qui m'ont pris l'honneur, ceux-là savent ce que je suis;

J'aurais auprès d'eux seuls un refuge contre la honte.

Ou bien conduisez-moi, ou faites venir votre maître,

Ah! Ne voulez-vous pas aller le trouver, par pitié?

Ainsi donc plus jamais je ne pourrai voir son visage,

Je n'entendrai sa voix! Pourtant je n'ai personne au monde

Sinon lui, maintenant qu'on a fait mourir mes amis.

Je suis trop déchiré, trop déchiré par la douleur.

     Hélas! mon ami, l'on le torture.

     Et moi, me voici à supplier

     En vain les valets de tes bourreaux.

     Ah! Mon ami, mon ami, tu cries;

     J'entends des cris; que ne suis-je sourd!

     Mon Dieu, je ne puis mourir ni vivre.

     Tout mon crime est d'avoir eu pitié.

Jaffier (II)

I leave without friends, banished, deprived of all my honour.

No one wants anything from me, now that I have lost all.

Where can I turn? For who would want to welcome a traitor

when even those whom my treachery saved will banish me?

This can't be happening. I want to talk to your master.

Those who have taken my honour, they know just what I am;

with them alone will I find a refuge against my shame.

Either lead me to your master, or have him brought to me.

Ah! Will you not go and find your master, out of pity?

Must it be, then, that I shall never again see his face,

never hear his voice? And yet I have no one in the world

apart from him, now that my friends have all been put to death.

I am being torn apart. I am being torn apart by pain.

> Alas! My friend, now they torture you.
>
> And I have been reduced to begging
>
> these servants and your hangmen in vain.
>
> Ah! My friend, my friend, how you cry out;
>
> I hear your screams; why am I not deaf?
>
> My God, I can neither die nor live.
>
> My crime was just to have shown pity.

Jaffier (III)

La mort vient me prendre. À present la honte est passée.

À mes yeux bientôt sans regard que la ville est belle!

Sans retour il faut m'éloigner des lieux des vivants.

On ne voit nulle aube où je vais, et nulle cité.

Jaffier (III)

Death is going to come for me. For now, the shame has passed.

To eyes that will soon go dark, how lovely is the city!

I must leave the land of the living, never to return.

There will be no dawn where I shall go, nor any city.

Violetta

Jour qui viens si beau, sourire suspendu

Soudain sur ma ville et ses mille canaux,

Combien aux humains qui reçoivent ta paix

    Voir le jour est doux!

Le sommeil encor jamais n'avait comblé

Tant que cette nuit mon cœur qui le buvait.

Mais il est venu, le jour doux à mes yeux

    Plus que le sommeil.

Voici que l'appel du jour tant attendu

Touche la cité parmi la pierre et l'eau.

Un frémissement dans l'air encor muet

    A surgi partout.

Ton bonheur est là, viens et vois ma cité.

Épouse des mères, vois bien loin, vois tout près

Tant de flots gonflés de murmures heureux

    Bénir ton éveil.

Sur la mer s'étend lentement la clarté.

La fête bientôt va combler nos désirs.

La mer calme attend. Qu'ils sont beaux sur la mer,

    Les rayons du jour!

Violetta

Loveliest day, now suddenly you're there,
on my city and its thousand canals;
those humans who now receive your smile
     see how sweet you are!

Never before have I slept, till last night!
My heart could drink and drink till sleep was dry.
Then the sweet day came, to my eyes
     lovelier than sleep!

The day so long awaited is now here,
touching the city of stone and water.
All around me is a gentle shiver
     in the still air.

Your bliss is there; come and see, my city.
Spouse of the sea, look far and look near.
So many high tides, such happy murmurs
     bless your awakening!

Daylight comes across the sea slowly.
Soon the feast will fulfil every desire.
The calm sea waits. How lovely on this sea
     are the rays of day!

SELECTED PROSE OF
SIMONE WEIL

Conte: Les Lutins du feu

Le bal allait, allait. . . . Les lutins sautaient leur joyeuse sarabande, plus haut, toujours plus haut. Les robes de lumière se frôlaient, rouges, jaunes, orange doré, projetant tout autour des lueurs fantastiques. Ils dansaient, les lutins de flamme, sur les bûches craquantes et le bois fendu, ils dansaient avec ivresse, bondissant et s'entrechoquant.

Il dansait, il dansait toujours, le peuple joyeux des « Phlogos », conduit par le plus grand, l'empereur, le « Mégistos ». Ils sautaient en le suivant, s'arrêtant parfois pour baiser ses pieds brûlants.

Il dansait, il dansait toujours, le people des âmes candides, des âmes des enfants qui ne sont pas encore nés; attendant leur tour d'être des hommes, les lutins se poursuivaient sur les bûches crépitantes.

Tout à coup, une grande lueur s'éleva, et tous jetèrent de brûlantes étincelles: au-dessus du feu flambant, une flamme avait élevé sa tête altière. Et, dans les crépitements, on entendit ces mots: « Phaidros Mégistos estin. » « Phaidros est Mégistos. »

Et la tête brillante de Phaidros s'illumina de fierté, tandis que tous, petits et grands, lui baisaient humblement les pieds, lui demandant: « Quel est ton bon plaisir? »

Tale: The Fairies of the Fire

The ball was going on and on and on. . . . The Fairies were leaping their joyful saraband: higher, ever higher. The garments of light rubbed against each other, red, yellow, golden orange, projecting the most fantastic lights all around. They were dancing, these Fairies of Flame, in the cracking logs and the split wood, they were dancing with intoxication, leaping up and crashing down.

They were dancing, they were still dancing, the joyful people of the 'Phlogos', led by the greatest of them all, the Emperor, the 'Megistos'. They leapt up as they followed him, sometimes stopping to kiss his burning feet.

They were dancing, they were still dancing, the people of the bright souls, of the souls of children who have not yet been born; waiting for their turn to become men, the Fairies were chasing each other on the crackling logs.

All of a sudden, a great light arose, and each one of them threw off burning sparks: above the blazing fire, one flame had lifted its haughty head. And, among the crackling wood, these words were heard: 'Phaidros Megistos estin'. 'Phaidros is Megistos'.

And the brilliant head of Phaidros lit up with pride, while everyone, small and great, humbly kissed his feet, asking him: 'What is your good pleasure?'

Il donna alors la main à sa belle fiancée, Chrysè à la robe d'or, et dansa une « orchèsis », la danse la plus exquise des Phlogos, où l'on ne distinguait que des tourbillons de flammes bleues, rouges ou dorées, où l'œil ne pouvait les suivre, où tous se confondaient dans une poussière enflammée.

Tout à coup, tout devint obscure, et une voix sanglotante cria en crépitant: «Phaidros Mégistos n'est plus! Phaidros Mégistos est mort!»

La danse cessa, il n'y eut plus que des sautillements saccadés; tous laissèrent là leurs couleurs brillantes et revêtirent leurs robes de deuil, d'un bleu livide. Ils pleuraient silencieusement des larmes d'or.

Après quelque temps, tous recommencèrent à danser, sauf Chrysè, ayant à leur tête le lutin Képhalè.

Mais par instants, au milieu des éclats de rire, des sanglots désespérés se faisaient entendre.

Soudain, des centaines d'étincelles sanglantes s'abattirent sur les danseurs, lancées avec une telle force qu'elles les obligèrent à se prosterner. Tous devinrent livides de peur. Quand tout d'un coup, on vit derrière une bûche la tête du lutin Klétès, qui portait le talisman de Phaidros. Car vous savez bien, mes enfants, que tout Phlogos porte sous sa robe le talisman qui lui donne sa hauteur, sa couleur, sa beauté, et que le vol en est puni de mort.

He then gave his hand to his beautiful fiancée, Chryse of the golden robe, and danced an 'orchesis', the most exquisite dance of the Phlogos, where all that could be seen was whirlwinds of blue, red or golden flames, until the eye could no longer follow them as they all blended together into a fiery dust.

All of a sudden, everything became dark and a sobbing voice crackled out: 'Phaidros Megistos is no more! Phaidros Megistos is dead!'

The dance came to a halt with only the odd spark here and there; everyone abandoned their brilliant colours and once more put on their mourning robes of livid blue. Silently they wept tears of gold.

After some time, they all began to dance again, apart from Chryse, with the Fairy Kephalos at their head.

But at times, among the bursts of laughter, some desperate sobbing made itself heard.

Suddenly, hundreds of sparks of blood came crashing down on the dancers, thrown with such force that they had to prostrate themselves. They all became livid with fear. And then, all at once, the head of the Fairy Kletos could be seen behind a log. He was carrying the talisman of Phaidros. For you should know, my children, that every Phlogos wears under their robe the talisman that grants them their height, their colour, their beauty. To steal a talisman is punishable by death.

« A-t-il volé le cadavre? » s'écria avec horreur Chrysè en s'avançant vers la bûche. Mais les étincelles l'obligèrent à reculer.

Et tous, blêmes, entendirent le bruit d'une lutte acharnée. Et tout à coup s'éleva une ombre d'un bleu livide, tandis que, fermant les yeux, tous s'écriaient: « Le fantôme de Phaidros! » Quand ils les rouvrirent, l'apparition avait disparu.

Tout, alentour, était plongé dans l'ombre. Seules, les cendres étaient rouges.

Bientôt, les étincelles cessèrent, et les Phlogos crièrent miracle: car Phaidros apparaissait, plus brillant que jamais.

Éméra, en effet, l'avait étourdi, mais non tué, et lui avait pris son talisman. Quand il reprit ses sens, ils se battirent; Phaidros, dépouillé de sa robe, dut fuir un instant vers le bal, mais bientôt se jeta sur Éméra, et l'égorgea.

Phaidros se jeta dans les bras de sa belle fiancée à larobe d'or (ce qui est le mariage des lutins) et ils dansèrent une « orchèsis » endiablée, allant plus vite que le vent, jetant des. étincelles, où l'on ne pouvait pas les distinguer, où ils étincelaient, voilés par une poussière d'or.

'Did he steal the body?' cried Chryse with horror, advancing to the log. But the sparks made her retreat.

And all of them turned pale as they heard the noise of a fierce battle. And all of a sudden there arose a shadow of livid blue, while, closing their eyes, they all cried out: 'The ghost of Phaidros!' When they opened their eyes again, the apparition had vanished.

Everything around them was plunged into shadow. Only the cinders were red.

Soon, the sparks ceased, and the Phlogos cried that it was a miracle: for Phaidros was approaching, more brilliant than ever.

Emera, in fact, had stunned but not killed him, and had taken his talisman. When he came back to his senses, they fought; Phaidros, stripped of his robe, had had to flee the ball for an instant, but soon he threw himself upon Emera, and cut his throat.

Phaidros threw himself into the arms of his beautiful fiancée of the golden robe (which means marriage to the Fairies) and together they danced a furious 'orchesis', going faster than the wind, throwing out sparks that hid them from view, and so they sparkled, veiled by a golden dust.

Le conte des six cygnes dans Grimm

Parmi les plus belles pensées de Platon sont celles qu'il a trouvées par la méditation des mythes. Qui sait si de nos mythes aussi il n'y aurait pas des idées à tirer? Choisissons-en un presque au hasard parmi les contes de Grimm, et prenons-le comme objet, en ayant soin de dire, comme Socrate: je dirai comme vrai tout ce que je vais dire.

Un roi tenait cachés dans la forêt ses six fils et sa fille, craignant pour eux la haine de leur belle-mère, qui était magicienne. Elle arrive pourtant à trouver les six fils, et jetant sur eux six chemises de soie enchantées, elle les transforma en cygnes. Elle ignorait l'existence de leur sœur. Celle-ci, partie à leur recherche, les rencontra au moment où, comme ils en avaient le pouvoir un quart d'heure chaque jour, ils reprenaient la forme humaine. Elle les quitta, crainte des voleurs, non sans avoir appris par eux leur seule chance de salut: ils reprendraient la forme humaine quand elle jetterait sur eux six chemises d'anémones cousues par elle en six années: six années pendant lesquelles elle ne devrait ni rire ni parler. Elle se mit à coudre aussitôt. Passa un roi qui la trouva belle: à ses questions point de réponse. Il la prit pour femme cependant, et elle eut de lui un fils. La mère du roi le fit enlever, accusa la reine de sa mort: les accusations la trouvèrent muette. De même pour le second

The Tale of the Six Swans in Grimm

Among the most beautiful thoughts of Plato are those that he found by meditation upon myths. Who knows if there might not be ideas that could be drawn from our myths as well? Let's choose at random from the tales of Grimm, and let's take one of them for our subject, being careful to say along with Socrates: I shall say what is true in all that I shall say.

A King was keeping his six sons and his daughter hidden in the forest, fearful of their stepmother's hatred for them. She was a magician. She managed to find the six sons, however, and, throwing on them six enchanted silk shirts, she transformed them into swans. She had no idea of their sister's existence. This sister, having gone in search of them, met them at the very moment when they returned to their human form, as they had the power to do for a quarter of an hour every day. She left them, fearing thieves, but not without having learned from them their one chance of salvation: they would return to human form when she threw at them six anemone shirts, sewn by her over six years: six years in which she was to neither laugh nor speak. She at once began to sew. There came by a King who found her beautiful: his questions received no reply. He took her as his wife anyway and she had a son by him. The King's mother had the son kidnapped and accused the Queen of his murder: the accusations found her unwilling to speak. The same happened with the second son; the

fils; de même pour le troisième. Quoiqu'il arrive autour d'elle, elle ne fait que coudre en silence. Le roi, qui l'aime pourtant, doit la condamner à mort; le jour où elle monte sur le bûcher est aussi le dernier des six ans. Comme on va y porter le feu, surviennent six cygnes blancs: elle jette sur eux les six chemises, et, ses frères délivrés, elle peut enfin se disculper. Ceux-ci vécurent auprès d'elle et du roi, le plus jeune ayant seulement une aile à la place du bras, parce qu'une manche manquait à la chemise d'anémones.

« Ce n'est pas là un conte, mais un discours », dirait Platon. Il nous faut penser cette femme comme étant au moment présent sur le point de jeter sur six cygnes six chemises d'anémones. Par le même moyen qui les a perdus, ses frères pourront être sauvés; comme ils ont été transformés, sans qu'il y eût de leur faute, ils reprennent leur première forme par le mérite d'autrui. Sans doute, s'ils avaient été enchantés pour une faute par eux commise, ils auraient dû subir l'épreuve qui les aurait délivrés; dans le conte, ils ont reçu le mal du dehors, ils reçoivent le bien du dehors aussi: l'on pourrait dire que tout cela n'intéresse que les corps. Mais le conte n'est pas le même que si l'épreuve de leur sœur avait été de chercher, par exemple, une plante magique: car la plante les aurait sauvés, et non leur sœur. Pour sauver les frères perdus par des chemises de soie, il faut des chemises d'anémones: mais elles n'ont qu'en apparence une vertu salutaire. Le salut des frères n'est pas là: leur sœur doit, pour les sauver,

same with the third. No matter what was going on around her, all she did was to sew in silence. The King, even though he loved her, had to condemn her to death; the day when she climbed onto the scaffold was also the last day of the six years. Just as the wood was about to be lit, six white swans arrived: she threw the six shirts onto them and, now that her brothers had been released, she was finally able to prove her innocence. Her brothers lived with her and the King, although the youngest still had a wing instead of an arm, because his anemone shirt only had one sleeve.

'This is not a tale but a discourse', Plato would say. We need to consider this woman at the very moment when she is about to throw six anemone shirts at the six swans. Her brothers can be saved by the same means by which they were lost; just as they were transformed through no fault of their own, so they can resume their original form by the merit of somebody else. Doubtless, if they had been enchanted for a fault that they had committed, they would have had to submit to an ordeal that would have saved them; in the tale, they received the evil from outside, and they also receive the good from outside: we can say that all of this concerns only their bodies. But here is a different tale from one in which the sister's ordeal had been to find, for example, a magic plant: for then it is the plant that would have saved them, and not their sister. To save the brothers who had been lost through silk shirts, anemone shirts are necessary: but they only *appear* to have a salvific virtue. This is not where the brothers' salvation is to be found: their

pendant six ans, ne pas rire et ne pas parler. Ici l'abstention pure agit. L'amour du roi, les accusations de sa mère rendent l'épreuve plus difficile; mais sa vraie vertu n'est pas là. Il faut qu'elle soit difficile: l'on ne fait rien sans effort; mais sa vertu est en elle-même. La tâche de coudre six chemises ne fait que fixer son effort et l'empêcher d'agir: car tous les actes lui sont impossibles si elle doit la mener à bout, excepté parler et rire. Le néant d'action possède donc une vertu. Cette idée rejoint le plus profond de la pensée orientale. Agir n'est jamais difficile: nous agissons toujours trop et nous répandons sans cesse en actes désordonnés. Faire six chemises avec des anémones, et se taire: c'est là notre seul moyen d'acquérir de la puissance. Les anémones ici ne représentent pas, comme on pourrait croire, l'innocence en face de la soie des chemises enchantées; quoique sans doute celui qui s'occupe six ans de coudre des anémones blanches n'est distrait par rien; ce sont des fleurs parfaitement pures; mais surtout les anémones sont presque impossibles à coudre en chemise, et cette difficulté empêche aucune autre action d'altérer la pureté de ce silence de six ans. La seule force en ce monde est la pureté; tout ce qui est sans mélange est un morceau de vérité. Jamais des étoffes chatoyantes n'ont valu un beau diamant. Les fortes architectures sont de belle pierre pure, de beau bois pur, sans artifice. Quand l'on ne ferait, comme méditation, que suivre pendant une minute l'aiguille des secondes sur le cadran d'une montre, ayant pour objet l'aiguille

sister has to save them by neither laughing nor speaking for six years. Here pure abstention is in play. The love of the King and the accusations of his mother make the ordeal more difficult; but this is not where its true virtue is to be found. It *has* to be difficult: nothing can be done without effort; but its virtue lies in itself. The task of sewing six shirts only fixes her effort and prevents her from acting: for every act is impossible for her if she is to fulfil her task, even speaking and laughing. The negation of action therefore possesses a virtue. This idea brings in the most profound thinking of the East. To act is never difficult: we always act too much and we constantly spread ourselves out in disordered acts. To make six shirts out of anemones, and to remain silent: this is our only means of gaining power. The anemones do not represent, as we might believe, innocence in opposition to the silk of the enchanted shirts; although anybody who can keep themselves busy for six years by sewing white shirts is distracted by nothing; these are perfectly pure flowers; but above all anemones are almost impossible to sew into shirts, and this difficulty allows no other action to alter the purity of this silence of six years. The only force in this world is purity; everything that is unadulterated is part of the truth. Shimmering materials have never had the value of a beautiful diamond. Great architecture consists of beautiful pure stone and beautiful pure wood, without any artifice. If all you do is to follow, as a meditation, for one minute the second hand of a watch, paying attention to the needle and to nothing else –

et rien d'autre, on n'aurait pas perdu son temps. La seule force et la seule vertu est de se retenir d'agir. Tout cela, vrai pour les âmes, ne l'est, dans le conte, pour les corps que parce qu'en cela seul consiste le mythe, de poser dans les corps une vérité qui est de l'âme. Le non-agir ne peut sur les corps que dans ce même pays où, selon Platon, des juges nus et morts jugent des âmes nues et mortes. Le drame du conte ne se passe que dans l'âme de l'héroïne: en elle les chemises de soie, en elle les chemises d'anémones; mais n'en sommes-nous pas avertis par le caractère magique de ces chemises, et le magique, n'est-ce pas l'expression dans notre corps de ce que seuls pourraient voir, au plus profond de notre âme, les juges nus et morts de Platon?

you will not have wasted your time. The only force and the only virtue is to restrain yourself from acting. All of this, true for the soul, is, in the tale, only true for the body because myth consists of this one thing: placing into the body a truth that comes from the soul. Non-acting on the body is possible only in the same country where, according to Plato, naked and dead judges pass judgement on naked and dead souls. The drama of the tale only takes place in the soul of the heroine: the silk shirts and the anemone shirts are within her; but are we not warned by the magical power of these shirts, and is not magic the expression in our body of that which, in the very depth of our soul, can only be seen by the naked and dead judges of Plato?

NOTES

Poetry

À une jeune fille riche/To a Rich Girl

Written in 1922 for Suzanne Gauchon (later Suzanne Aron) when Simone Weil was at the Lycée Fénelon.

- Clymene [1.1]: many women in Greek mythology are called Clymene, including the mother of Prometheus and the wife of Ophion, first ruler of Olympus, who was cast down to Tartarus with her husband. The name is probably best seen as a literary device rather than a cipher.

- *sous* [6.6]: the *sou* is a notional French term for a coin of little value, so the reference is to women selling their flesh cheaply.

- greenhouse [8.1]: the French *serre* can also mean 'hothouse'. It is possible to interpret the *serre* as a metaphor for Weil's parents. Anne Carson (using a different metaphor) describes how Weil's life was 'caught in the net of her parents' care' and how she took 'lunges

through the net' until she finally escaped by dying
(Carson 2006: 223). Weil frequently relied on her parents
for both material and spiritual support: her mother
accompanied her to her first teaching post, for example,
and both parents met her in Barcelona when she was
invalided from the front in the Spanish Civil War and
oversaw her convalescence. Weil's death took her parents
completely by surprise, because her letters from London
had been so full of energy, assuring them that she was
eating well and praising traditional English dishes such
as roast lamb with mint sauce.

Vers lus au Goûter de la Saint Charlemagne/ Verses Read at the Feast of Saint Charlemagne

Written for recitation at the traditional Feast on 30 January 1926,
when Weil was a pupil at the Lycée Henri-IV in Paris.

- Charlemagne (748–814) [Title]: 'Charles the Great' was
  King of the Franks from 768, King of the Lombards
  from 774 and first Holy Roman Emperor from 800. He
  was a powerful warlord who devoted great energy to
  spreading the Catholic faith and was popularly revered
  as a saint after his death, with a legend growing up that
  he was only sleeping and would one day rise to save
  France. His canonization by an anti-Pope was overturned

by the Church, so that he is not officially a saint, but
we have maintained his saintly status in translation.
Weil would have known the massive equestrian statue
of Charlemagne in front of Notre-Dame Cathedral in
Paris, indicative of the role that he played in the French
imaginary of her time.

- clarity [2.7]: the noun *clarté* signifies a light that is both
physical and intellectual, as befits a follower of Plato. It
has been translated in various ways. It is used in the lyric
spoken by Violetta at the end of *Venice Saved*, to indicate
day breaking on the Adriatic.

- glaive [3.2]: a type of poleaxe.

- Durandal and Joyeuse [6.5]: legendary swords associated
with Roland and Charlemagne respectively. Roland (d.
778) is the protagonist of the anonymous eleventh-century
Old French epic *La Chanson de Roland* [The Song of
Roland], the earliest extant work in French Literature, in
which he dies a noble death in battle against Muslim forces
in Spain, while commanding Charlemagne's rear guard.

- saint [12.5]: this unnamed figure might be the fifth-
century Saint Genevieve, patron saint of Paris, whose
prayers were believed to have twice saved the city from
invasion. (The Lycée Henri-IV is on the Montagne
Sainte-Geneviève in Paris.)

Éclair/Lightning

Written in 1929.

- cleansed of each dream [1.4]: Weil used the metaphor of dreaming to show how the imagination (of which she had a negative view), born of the self and its inherent self-expansion, distorts reality; it is the opposite of attention, which is creative. In *Venice Saved*, the conspirators are called 'dreamers' for this reason, seeing Venice and its inhabitants as merely objects of their conquest and desires.

- There is a translation, 'Illumination', by Carol Cosman in Bankier et al. (1976: 21).

Prométhée/Prometheus

Written in 1937, Weil sent this poem to the writer Paul Valéry. He found it too didactic, despite praising certain aspects. Prometheus was a Titan in Greek mythology who gave the gift of fire to humans. Zeus punished him by having him chained to a rock and sending an eagle each day to eat his liver. Weil made frequent reference to him in the *Cahiers* [notebooks] (cf. NB 450) and wrote two sustained reflections on him (IC 56–9 and 60–73).

- trembling with lassitude [1.3]: Valéry did not like 'tremblant de lassitude'. (Creative writing tutors frequently advise students to avoid abstraction.) We have therefore stayed close to it as an exercise in loyalty in translation.

- affliction [6.10]: the noun *malheur* is rendered as 'affliction' by Weil's translators and is used by her to signify something more than suffering: the total destruction of the soul (physical, social and psychological at once), such as experienced by Jesus on the cross. (Emma Craufurd notes the word's 'sense of inevitability and doom' (WG 67n)). It is a key concept in her later metaphysical thinking and an important tool in her political philosophy: she identifies the workers' condition, their oppression and alienation, with the complete emptiness generated by affliction (see, for example, 'Analysis of Oppression' in SWA 147–77).

À un jour/To a Day

Written in 1938. Weil also sent this poem to Valéry and was disappointed not to receive a reply.

- And fill the heart with a void [15.9]: the idea of filling with void is puzzling, but for Weil the 'void' is the space that is created when we give up our natural desire of interfering with the world through the activities of the self. It is the 'dark night of the soul', as depicted by Saint John of the Cross, which can lead to destruction, but is also the only way to reach salvation from the pull of 'gravity'.

La mer/The Sea

The first of four poems written in 1941–2 when Weil was resident in Vichy France, the collaborationist state formed in the south after France had fallen to German invasion in 1940.

- attention, without desire [2.4]: for Weil, true attention is always without desire, because attention allows its object to be, while desire possesses and distorts.
- afflicted [5.1]: translating *malheureux*. See the second note to 'Promethée'/'Prometheus' above.

Nécessité/Necessity

Written in 1941–2. There is a translation by Joan Dargan (1991: 91). For a full discussion of Weil on necessity and obedience, see McCullough (2014: 123–70).

- the naked soul [4.3]: references to nakedness in the poems have been linked by Roberto Carifi to the theme of spiritual nudity in medieval mystics such as Meister Eckhart (1998: 8–11). Both the judges and the judged

at the end of 'The Tale of the Six Swans in Grimm'
are naked.

Les astres/The Stars

Written in 1941–2. The existence of four variants of the last line
shows how Weil's poetry should be seen as work in progress.
There is a translation by William Burford (SWR 409).

- their divine fires [10]: in Plato's *Timaeus*, the gods are for
  the most part stars made of fire (40a).

La porte/The Gate

Written in 1941–2.

- The Gate [Title]: the French noun 'porte' can mean both
  'gate' and 'door' in English. (William Burford renders the
  title as 'Threshold' in his translation (SWR 408), while
  David Raper also opts for 'The Gate' (GTG 7).)

- Waiting [2.2]: the French present participle 'Attendant'
  recalls the (editorial) title of the collection of Weil's writing
  Attente de Dieu – which has appeared in English translation
  as *Waiting on God*, *Waiting for God* and *Awaiting God* –
  and includes the notions of both waiting and attending.
  Attente is the French term used by Weil for 'attention'.

Four excerpts from *Venice Saved*

Weil worked on *Venice Saved* from 1940 until her death, in very difficult conditions. There is controversy among historians about what actually happened in the supposed 1618 conspiracy against Venice (see Norwich 2003: 522). Weil's source was the 1674 historical fiction by the Abbé de Saint-Réal (César Vichard), on which Thomas Otway based his 1682 tragedy *Venice Preserv'd*, a play that Weil knew and to which she owes her title. The speeches are taken from Act 3 Scene 4 (PVS 121, 122, 133, 133/VS 104, 105, 112, 113, respectively).

Jaffier I–III

The mercenary Jaffier has betrayed a conspiracy to topple Venice, for which his life has been spared, but he has been forced to watch his companions, including his beloved friend Pierre, arrested and taken to horrific torture and death. He speaks surrounded by taunting Venetians, struggling in his affliction 'like a butterfly pinned alive into an album' (WG 81), and eventually joins what is left of the conspiracy in order to fight to the death.

Violetta

Violetta is the daughter of the Secretary of the Council of Ten. Her words end the play and celebrate Venice's Marriage to the

Sea. She is unaware of the deaths of the conspirators and of how she has narrowly escaped horrific violence at their hands. Weil struggled to get a definitive version of this poem, which imitates the Sapphic stanza (with the added rhyme).

Selected prose

Conte: Les Lutins du feu/Tale: The Fairies of the Fire

Weil wrote this story during the winter of 1920–1 aged eleven.

- The Fairies of the Fire [Title]: the noun 'Lutin' offers several translation possibilities. Dictionaries suggest 'goblin', 'sprite' and 'imp', but we chose 'Fairy' – which we capitalize – because its connotations capture the beauty of Weil's creatures as well as their savagery.

- 'Megistos' [l. 7]: Weil gives her characters Greek names that sum up the role that they play in the story and contribute to its mysterious, esoteric nature, especially for readers with no Greek. She also uses the Greek verb *estin* [is] in terminal position. Her brother André was learning ancient Greek and teaching her. We have made slight alterations to the spelling of some of the names but did not relocalize them. The terms have the following meanings in English:

Chryse: golden

Emera: day

estin: is

Kephalos: head

Kletos: welcome

Megistos: chief

Orchesis: dance

Phaidros: bright

Phlogos: flame

Le conte des six cygnes dans Grimm/ The Tale of the Six Swans in Grimm

This essay was a philosophy *topo* [short assignment] written for Alain (Émile-Auguste Chartier) at the Lycée Henri-IV and dated November 1925, when Weil was preparing for university entrance. The source story 'Die sechs Schwäne' [The Six Swans] first appeared in a collection of German folk tales made by Jacob and Wilhelm Grimm in 1812. A recommended English translation is by Jack Zipes (Grimm and Grimm 2007: 220–4).

- 'The naked and dead judges pass judgement on naked and dead souls' [l.56]: as described by Socrates in Plato's *Gorgias* (523e–527a). Robin Waterfield comments on this Platonic myth: 'As usual, Plato interweaves his own invention with folk tradition and mystical elements drawn from Pythagoreanism and Orphism' (1994: 165n).

FURTHER READING

We offer an introduction to Simone Weil and extensive suggestions on literature about her life and thought in our translation of her play, published in 2019 by Bloomsbury as *Venice Saved*. Two excellent overviews of Weil are by Stephen Plant (2007) and Palle Yourgrau (2011). Recent studies by Eric O. Springsted (2021) and Robert Zaretsky (2021) show Weil's continuing relevance to the world. The essay on Weil by Deborah Nelson (2017) in her study of six twentieth-century women is subtle and profound. The monographs by Joan Dargan (1999), Katherine Brueck (1995) and Marie Cabaud Meaney (2007) engage in different ways with Weil and literature. The edited collection by Eric O. Springsted and John Dunaway (1996) contains useful contributions concerning Weil on language and aesthetics. For those new to Weil's thought, two good places to start are the anthology *Gravity and Grace* (2003) and *Waiting for God* (1973), which is available in several translations.

BIBLIOGRAPHY

Allen, D. (1985), 'George Herbert and Simone Weil', *Religion & Literature*, 17 (2): 17–34.

Angelus Silesius [1657] (1986), *The Cherubinic Wanderer*, trans. M. Shrady, New York: Paulist.

Aquinas, T. (1947), *Summa Theologica*, trans. Fathers of the Dominican Province, London: R.T. Washbourne.

Armitage, S. (2021), *A Vertical Art*, Oxford: Oxford University Press.

Attridge, D. (2004), *The Singularity of Literature*, London: Routledge.

Bakewell, S. (2016), *At the Existentialist Café*, London: Chatto and Windus.

Bankier, J., C. Cosman, D. Earnshaw, J. Keefe, D. Lashgari and K. Weaver, eds (1976), *The Other Voice: Twentieth-Century Women's Poetry in Translation*, London: Norton.

Barber, M. (2000), *The Cathars*, London: Pearson.

Barnstone, W. (1972), 'Introduction', in John of the Cross *The Poems of Saint John of the Cross*, trans. W. Barnstone, 9–36, New York: New Directions.

Barnstone, W. (1993), *The Poetics of Translation*, New Haven: Yale University Press.

Benfey, C. (2005), 'Introduction: A Tale of Two *Iliads*', in S. Weil and R. Bespaloff, *War and the Iliad*, trans. M. McCarthy, vii–xxiii, New York: New York Review Books.

Boase-Beier, J. (2019), *Translation and Style*, London: Routledge.

Boase-Beier, J. and M. Holman (1999), *The Practices of Literary Translation*, Manchester: St. Jerome.

Boase-Beier, J. and M. de Vooght, eds (2019), *Poetry of the Holocaust*, Todmorden: Arc.

Brueck, K. T. (1995), *The Redemption of Tragedy: The Literary Vision of Simone Weil*, New York: SUNY Press.

Cabaud Meaney, M. (2007), *Simone Weil's Apologetic Use of Literature: Her Christological Interpretations of Ancient Greek Texts*, Oxford: Oxford University Press.

Cameron, S. (2007), *Impersonality: Seven Essays*, Chicago: University of Chicago Press.

Caprioglio Panizza, S. (2022), *The Ethics of Attention: Engaging the Real with Iris Murdoch and Simone Weil*, New York: Routledge.

Carifi, R. (1998), 'Introduzione: L'etica dell'abbandono', in S. Weil, *Poesie*, trans. R. Carifi, 7–21, Milano: Mondadori.

Carson, A. (2006), *Decreation*, London: Jonathan Cape.

Catling, J. (2007), 'Rilke's "Left-Handed Lyre": Multilingualism and the Poetics of Possibility', *The Modern Languages Review*, 102 (4): 1084–104.

Cavell, S. (2002), *Must We Mean What We Say?* Cambridge: Cambridge University Press.

Chase, M. (1995), 'Translator's Note', in P. Hadot, *Philosophy as a Way of Life*, vi–viii, Oxford: Blackwell.

Coetzee, J. M. (2003), *Elizabeth Costello*, London: Vintage.

Crane, T. (2015), 'Consciousness and Castles', *Times Literary Supplement*, January 30.

Dargan, J. (1999), *Simone Weil: Thinking Poetically*, New York: SUNY Press.

Davis, L. (2021), *Essays Two*, London: Penguin.

Deguy, M., trans. (2008), 'Seamus Heaney: Pylos: Poème lu par Michel Deguy', *Poésie*, 122–3: 52.

Dickinson, E. (1999), *The Poems of Emily Dickinson*, Cambridge, MA: Belknap Press.

Fiori, G. (1989), *Simone Weil: An Intellectual Biography*, trans. J. R. Berrigan, Athens: University of Georgia Press.

Grimm, J. and W. Grimm (2007), *The Complete Fairy Tales*, trans. J. Zipes, London: Vintage.

Hadot, P. (1995), *Philosophy as a Way of Life*, Oxford: Blackwell.

Herbert, G. (1885), *The Canterbury Poets: George Herbert*, ed. William Sharp, London: Walter Scott.

Housden, R., ed. (2009), *For Lovers of God Everywhere*, Carlsbad: Hay House.

Huston, N. (2005), *Longings and Belongings*, Toronto: McArthur and Company.

Jameson, F. (1981), *The Political Unconscious: Narrative as a Socially Symbolic Act*, Ithaca: Cornell University Press.

John of the Cross (1972), *The Poems of Saint John of the Cross*, trans. W. Barnstone, New York: New Directions.

Kafka, F. [1925] (1994), *The Trial*, trans. I. Parry, London: Penguin.

Klagge, J., ed. (2001), *Wittgenstein: Biography and Philosophy*, Cambridge: Cambridge University Press.

Kotva, S. (2020), 'The Occult Mind of Simone Weil', *Philosophical Investigations*, 43 (1–2): 122–41.

Kraus, C. (2000), *Aliens and Anorexia*, Cambridge, MA: MIT Press.

La Chanson de Roland (1990), Paris: Livre de Poche.

Large, D. (2014), 'On the Work of Philosopher-Translators', in J. Boase-Beier, A. Fawcett and P. Wilson (eds), *Literary Translation: Redrawing the Boundaries*, 182–203, Basingstoke: Palgrave Macmillan.

Little, J. P. (1996), 'Simone Weil and the Limits of Language', in E. O. Springsted and J. M. Dunaway (eds), *The Beauty that Saves: Essays on Aesthetics and Language in Simone Weil*, 39–55, Macon: Mercer University Press.

Lodge, D. (1988), *Nice Work*, London: Secker and Warburg.

Lorde, A. (2017), *Your Silence Will Not Protect You*, London: Silver Press.

Mac Cumhaill, C. and R. Wiseman (2022), *Metaphysical Animals*, London: Chatto and Windus.

Magee, B. (2021), 'Pensées by Bryan Magee', *New Statesman*, 30 July–19 August: 48–61.

Marx, K. (2022), *Evening Hour*, trans. P. Wilson, Todmorden: Arc.

McCullough, L. (2014), *The Religious Philosophy of Simone Weil*, London: I.B. Tauris.

McCullough, L. (2018), 'Simone Weil', in C. D. Rodkey and J. E. Miller (eds), *The Palgrave Handbook of Radical Theology*, 459–72, Basingstoke: Palgrave Macmillan.

McKee, R. (1999), *Story*, London: Methuen.

McKinney, M. (2005), 'Pillow Book Talk', *Meanjin*, 64 (4): 54–9.

Monk, R. (2001), 'Philosophical Biography: The Very Idea', in J. Klagge (ed.), *Wittgenstein: Biography and Philosophy*, 3–15, Cambridge: Cambridge University Press.

Montaigne, M. de (2004), *The Essays: A Selection*, trans. M. A. Screech, London: Penguin.

Murdoch, I. (1997), 'The Fire and the Sun: Why Plato Banished the Artists', in *Existentialists and Mystics*, 386–463, London: Penguin.

Nelson, D. (2017), *Tough Enough*, Chicago: The University of Chicago Press.

Nevin, T. R. (1991), *Simone Weil: Portrait of a Self-Exiled Jew*, Chapel Hill: University of North Carolina Press.

Nicolaus, M. (1973), 'Note on the Translation', in M. Nicolaus (ed. and trans.), *K. Marx Grundrisse: Foundations of the Critique of Political Economy*, 65–6, Harmondsworth: Penguin.

Noel-Tod, J., ed. (2019), *The Penguin Book of the Prose Poem*, London: Penguin.

Nolan, M. (2021), 'Lines of Dissent', *New Statesman*, 5–11 February: 58.

Norwich, J. J. (2003), *A History of Venice*, London: Penguin.

Olsson, K. (2019), *The Weil Conjectures*, London: Bloomsbury.

Pétrement, S. (1976), *Simone Weil: A Life*, trans. R. Rosenthal, London: Mowbrays.

Plant, S. (2007), *The SPCK Introduction to Simone Weil*, London: SPCK.

Plato [c. 380 BCE] (1994a), *Symposium*, trans. R. Waterfield, Oxford: Oxford University Press.

Plato [c. 380 BCE] (1994b), *Gorgias*, trans. R. Waterfield, Oxford: Oxford University Press.

Plato [c. 380 BCE] (1998), *The Republic*, trans. R. Waterfield, Oxford: Oxford University Press.

Plato [c. 380 BCE] (2008), *Timaeus* and *Critias*, trans. R. Waterfield, Oxford: Oxford University Press.

Prawer, S. S. (1976), *Karl Marx and World Literature*, Oxford: Oxford University Press.

Pseudo-Dionysius (1987), *The Complete Works*, trans. C. Luibheid, New York: Paulist.

Pym, A. (2007), 'Philosophy and Translation', in P. Kuhiwczak and K. Littau (eds), *A Companion to Translation Studies*, 24–44, Clevedon, Buffalo, Toronto: Multilingual Matters.

Rawling, P. and P. Wilson, eds (2019), *The Routledge Handbook of Translation and Philosophy*, London: Routledge.

Rees, W., ed. (1980), *The Penguin Book of French Poetry 1820–1950*, London: Penguin.

Schwartz, R., trans. (forthcoming), *Simone Weil: The Need for Roots*, London: Penguin.

Scott, C. (2008), 'Our Engagement with Literary Translation', *In Other Words*, 32: 16–29.

Shakespeare, W. [1623] (2015), *Romeo and Juliet*, London: Penguin.

Shread, C. (2019), 'Translating Feminist Philosophers', in P. Rawling and P. Wilson (eds), *The Routledge Handbook of Translation and Philosophy*, 324–44, London: Routledge.

Springsted, E. O. (2021), *Simone Weil for the Twenty-First Century*, Notre Dame: University of Notre Dame Press.

Springsted, E. O. and J. M. Dunaway, eds (1996), *The Beauty that Saves: Essays on Aesthetics and Language in Simone Weil*, Macon: Mercer University Press.

Taleb, N. N. (2018), *Skin in the Game*, London: Allen Lane.

Valéry, P. (1954), 'Poetry and Abstract Thought', trans. C. Guenther, *The Kenyon Review*, 16 (2): 208–33.

Waterfield, R., trans. (1994), *Plato: Gorgias*, Oxford: Oxford University Press.

Waugh, R. (2021), 'Voicing a Life', *New Statesman*, 5–11 February: 51.

Weil, S. [1951] (1956), *The Notebooks of Simone Weil*, trans. A. Wills, 2 vols, London: Routledge.

Weil, S. (1957), *Intimations of Christianity among the Ancient Greeks*, trans. E. Chase Geissbuhler, London: Routledge.

Weil, S. (1965), *Seventy Letters*, trans. R. Rees, London: Oxford University Press.

Weil, S. [1955] (1968), *Poèmes suivis de Venise sauvée, Lettre de Paul Valéry*, Paris: Gallimard.

Weil, S. (1970), *First and Last Notebooks*, trans. R. Rees, London: Oxford University Press.

Weil, S. [1951] (1973), *Waiting for God*, trans. E. Craufurd, New York: Harper and Row.

Weil, S. (1977), *The Simone Weil Reader*, ed. G. A. Panichas, New York: David Mckay.

Weil, S. (1978), *Lectures on Philosophy*, trans. H. Price, Cambridge: Cambridge University Press.

Weil, S. (1982), *Gateway to God*, ed. D. Raper, New York: Crossroad.

Weil, S. (1999), *Œuvres*, ed. F. de Lussy, Paris: Gallimard.

Weil, S. [1955] (2001), *Oppression and Liberty*, trans. A. Wills and J. Petrie, London: Routledge.

Weil, S. [1951] (2002a), *Letter to a Priest*, trans. A. Wills, London: Routledge.

Weil, S. [1949] (2002b), *The Need for Roots*, trans. A. Wills, London: Routledge.

Weil S. [1947] (2003), *Gravity and Grace*, trans. E. Crawford and M. von der Ruhr, London: Routledge.

Weil, S. [1940] (2005), 'The Iliad, or The Poem of Force', in S. Weil and R. Bespaloff, *War and the Iliad*, trans. M. McCarthy, 3–37, New York: New York Review Books.

Weil, S. (2005), *Simone Weil: An Anthology*, ed. S. Miles, London: Penguin.

Weil, S. [Sylvie] (2009), *At Home with André and Simone Weil*, trans. B. Ivry, Evanston: Northwestern University Press.

Weil, S. [1940] (2014a), *On the Abolition of All Political Parties*, trans. S. Leys, New York: NYRB Classics.

Weil, S. (2014b), 'Some Reflections around the Concept of Value: On Valéry's Claim that Philosophy is Poetry', trans. E. O. Springsted, *Philosophical Investigations*, 37 (2): 105–12.

Weil, S. (2015), *Late Philosophical Writings*, ed. E. O. Springsted, Notre Dame: University of Notre Dame Press.

Weil, S. [1955] (2019), *Venice Saved*, ed. and trans. S. Panizza and P. Wilson, London: Bloomsbury.

Weil, S. [1937] (2020), 'The Power of Words', trans. R. Rees, in *The Power of Words*, 1–26, London: Penguin.

Weinberger, E. and O. Paz (1987), *19 Ways of Looking at Wang Wei*, London: Asphodel.

Wilson, P. (2018), 'Demanding the Impossible', in D. Large, M. Akashi, W. Józwikowska and E. Rose (eds), *Untranslatablity: Interdisciplinary Perspectives*, London: Routledge.

Wilson, P. (2021), 'Not Only Rivers and Mountains: Why Narrative Matters', *New Area Studies* 2: 7–38.

Wittgenstein, L. (1981), *Zettel*, trans. G. E. M. Anscombe, Oxford: Blackwell.

Wittgenstein, L. [1921] (1990), *Tractatus Logico-Philosophicus*, trans. C. K. Ogden [and F. Ramsey], London: Routledge.

Wittgenstein, L. (2009), *Philosophical Investigations*, trans. G. E. M. Anscombe, P. M. S. Hacker and J. Schulte, Oxford: Wiley-Blackwell.

Womack, P. (1993), 'What Are Essays For?', *English in Education*, 27 (2): 42–8.

Wright, C. (2016), *Literary Translation*, London: Routledge.

Yourgrau, P. (2011), *Simone Weil*, London: Reaktion Books.

Zaretsky, R. (2021), *The Subversive Simone Weil*, Chicago: University of Chicago Press.

Zipes, J. (2007), 'Once There Were Two Brothers Named Grimm', in J. Grimm and W. Grimm, *The Complete Fairy Tales*, trans. J. Zipes, xxviii–xlvi, London: Vintage.

INDEX

affliction   xv, 5, 25, 39, 40, 81,
    161, 162
Alain [Émile-Auguste Chartier]
    3, 12, 13, 46, 77, 166
Antigone, see under Sophocles
Armitage, Simon   xvi, 3
Assisi   18, 21
attention
    to beauty   30
    and desire   162
    to the divine   19
    exercises of   2, 42, 68
    and love   20
    to poetry   5, 22, 50, 54, 57,
        59
    and reality   27, 46, 49, 160
    and suffering   xiii, 80
    as a theme in Weil's
        philosophy   5, 29, 33, 34,
        54, 56, 163
    and translation   66–8

beauty, *see also* attention
    and detachment   45
    fading   12
    and indifference   32
    in Plato   22
    and poetry   4, 26, 36, 51, 57
    as a theme in Weil's
        philosophy   5, 17, 29
    in *Venice Saved*   22, 30, 37,
        40, 41
    of the world   30, 31, 36, 52

Beckett, Samuel   38
Benjamin, Walter   69
Bernanos, Georges   15
Bhagavad Gita   13, 27, 42,
    46–8, 51
Boase-Beier, Jean   xv n.2, 3, 71

Cabaud Meaney, Marie   47, 48,
    50 n.1
Camus, Albert   42, 43
Carifi, Roberto   6, 162
Carson, Anne   xii, 68, 157, 158
Catharism   25, 28, 29, 29 n.10,
    see also Christianity
Catholicism   11, 12, 16, 18, 20,
    23, 25, 28 n.9, 50, 64, 158,
    see also Christianity
Cavell, Stanley   3
Celan, Paul   3, 4
La Chanson de Roland   16, 159
Charlemagne   13, 14, 16,
    158, 159
Christ   11, 19, 23, 50, 80–2
Christianity   6, 12, 16, 18, 23–5,
    42, 47, 68
Coetzee, J. M.   34
crucifixion   23, 25, 26
Csikszentmihalyi, Mihaly   67

Dargan, Joan   xv, 32, 162
dark night of the soul   162
Davis, Lydia   65, 67, 76
decreation   28, 68, 82

Derrida, Jacques   144
Dickinson, Emily   2
Dionysus   23

eating   36, 46, 49, 50, 56
'Essay on the Concept of Reading'
        (Simone Weil)   58, 60
evil   31, 32, 151

Fascism   14, 15, 21, 22
Fiori, Gabriella   18, 22, 37, 40
friendship   39, 67

Ginsberg, Alan   9
Gnosticism   25, 28, 29
Grimm, Jacob and Wilhelm   xi,
        xvi, 77–9, 81, 82, 166

Hadot, Pierre   65
Heaney, Seamus   xii, 65
Heidegger, Martin   63
Herbert, George   xv, 19
    'Love' (poem)   19, 50–2, 56
the Holocaust   3, 4, 25 n.8
Homer   48, 69, 72, 73
    Iliad   15, 47, 49, 60, 61, 69

instrumental value   53, 55
intellect   17, 35, 52, 53

Judaism   xii, 8, 25

Kabbalah, *see* Luria, Isaac
Kafka, Franz   34, 36
Krishna   23, 64, 80

Lao-Tse   48
Large, Duncan   65, 69

Lawrence, T. E.   16, 17
Little, J. P.   56, 57
Lorde, Audre   7
Luria, Isaac   20
de Lussy, Florence   33, 34

McCullough, Lissa   2, 6 n.2, 18,
        29 n.10, 32, 32 n.12, 162
McKinney, Meredith   70
Madame Bovary (Gustave
        Flaubert)   67
Marx, Carl   4, 23, 65
metaphysics   5, 6, 26, 27, 30,
        36 n.15, 161
Modernism   38, 38 n.17, 60
Monk, Ray   2
Montaigne, Michel de   48, 76,
        77
Murdoch, Iris   1, 22 n.5
mysticism   11, 19–21, 27–9,
        42, 49
    and attention   33, 34
    experience   51
    in mystics such as Meister
        Eckhart   162
    and Plato   20
    and poetry   3 n.1, 19, 33, 51
    in Pseudo-Dionysius the
        Areopagite   35 n.14
    and translation   68
myth   78, 79, 81, 82
    Greek   24, 73, 157, 160

Nazism   xiii, 15, 80
necessity   5, 26, 29–32, 34, 46, 52,
        57, 162
The Need for Roots (Simone Weil)
        14, 41, 70

Nevin, Thomas R.   8, 21, 24, 26, 27, 30, 39

obedience   5, 30, 31, 49, 50, 162
Odin   23
Osiris   23

Pilgrim's Progress (John Bunyan)   13
Plato   5, 6, 20, 22, 27, 29, 46, 77, 78, 159, 166
    Gorgias   82, 166
    Republic   27, 70, 78
    Symposium   22, 27
    Timaeus   163
'The Power of Words' (Simone Weil)   72
'Prerequisite to Dignity of Labour' (Simone Weil)   61
Prometheus   23–5, 31, 33, 39, 157, 160
Proust, Marcel   48
    Du côté de chez Swann [Swann's Way]   67
Pythagoreans   48, 166

Racine, Jean   38, 48, 70
Republic, see under Plato
Rimbaud, Arthur   13, 48

Saint John of the Cross, *see* dark night of the soul
Saint Paul   13
Sanskrit   42, 47, 64
Schleiermacher, Friedrich   69
Schwarz, Ros   70
Second World War   14

Sei Shônagon (*The Pillow Book*)   70
Shakespeare, William   35, 48
silence   5, 56, 57, 79, 81
Socrates   22, 27, 78, 82, 166, *see also* Plato
'Some Reflections around the Concept of Value' (Simone Weil)   46, 54
Sophocles   46, 48
    Antigone   61, 79
Spanish Civil War   14, 15, 80, 158
'Spiritual Autobiography' (Simone Weil)   51
supernatural   6, 22, 25, 30, 52, 60, 61
Symposium, see under Plato

Taleb, N. N.   10
Thibon, Gustave   28 n.9, 71
time   5, 57, 62
Tolkien, J. R. R.   20
tragedy   55, 60
    Greek   23, 61
    Venice Saved   37, 38, 61, 164
transformation   28, 30, 33, 51, 53–6, 59, 62

Upanishads   36, 46, 49

Valéry, Paul   5, 7, 24, 26, 48, 53, 54, 57, 160, 161
Venice Saved   xi, xii, 37, 38, 159, 160, 164
    beauty in   17
    the sea in   30
    style of   xv, 4, 5, 18, 27, 38, 57
    transformation in   55

Weil's political thinking in
    11, 13, 14

waiting   33, 34, 57, 58, 66, 67,
    81, 163
Waugh, Rosemary   11
Wills, Arthur   70

Wittgenstein, Ludwig   1, 2, 63,
    72, 81

Yourgrau, Palle   12, 77

Zaretsky, Robert   12
Zipes, Jack   79